Finland

Frontispiece: **Northern lights**

Consultant: Ellen L. Marakowitz, Department of Anthropology,
Columbia University, New York, NY

Please note: All statistics are as up-to-date as possible at the time of publication.

Book production by The Design Lab

Library of Congress Cataloging-in-Publication Data
Names: Clark, Geri, 1970- author.
Title: Finland / by Geri Clark.
Description: [Revised edition]. | New York, NY : Children's Press, an imprint
    of Scholastic Inc., 2018. | Series: Enchantment of the world | Includes
    bibliographical references and index.
Identifiers: LCCN 2017054631 | ISBN 9780531130469 (library binding)
Subjects: LCSH: Finland—Juvenile literature.
Classification: LCC DL1012 .C63 2018 | DDC 948.97—dc23
LC record available at https://lccn.loc.gov/2017054631

Scholastic Inc., 557 Broadway, New York, NY 10012

1 2 3 4 5 6 7 8 9 10 R 28 27 26 25 24 23 22 21 20 19

Finland

BY GERI CLARK

Enchantment of the World™
Second Series

CHILDREN'S PRESS®

An Imprint of Scholastic Inc.

Contents

Left to right: **Snowy forest, pine grosbeak, Oulu, whooper swans, forestry**

CHAPTER I

Finland Today

IN 2017, FINLAND CELEBRATED ITS ONE HUNDREDTH anniversary as a republic. In that century, many things have changed, while some have stayed the same.

Just one hundred years ago, Finland had a traditional economy built on forestry and fishing. Today, Finland is a thoroughly modern nation with an economy based on high-tech industries. Once a place where people made a living by cutting down trees or fishing for perch or farming potatoes, Finland is now a place that leads the world in innovation. The cell phone was invented in Finland. The computer operating system Linux was born there. Video games played by millions of people all over the world were designed by Finns.

One hundred years ago, Finland was a brand-new country, free for the first time after a thousand years of rule by other nations. Today, it is a respected independent nation. As

Opposite: **People relax in Esplanade Park, which cuts through the heart of Helsinki, the capital of Finland. The park is popular for picnics and musical performances.**

- ✪ Capital
- ● Major city
- ○ City
- ▪ National park

a member of the European Union, Finland contributes to social and economic decisions and policies that are felt around the world.

One hundred years ago, many people in Finland could not read or write. Few people had more than a basic education. Today, Finland's education system stands out as one of the best in the world.

All of these changes were possible because of what stayed the same—the character and values of the Finnish people. Finns say they accomplished so much in so little time because of *sisu*. It's a word that has no direct translation to English. Finns use it to mean strength, determination, and perseverance. It's a quality that allows people to pick themselves up when things go wrong and start over again. It is the idea that being sensible and practical makes a people strong enough to withstand anything.

Sisu is what made it possible for Finns to never lose their national identity and to continue their fight for independence.

Sisu enabled Finland to build entire industries to pay off a massive war debt. Sisu allowed Finns to rebuild a failing economy. Sisu helped Finland stand up to the most powerful countries in the world, and sisu gets Finns in the northern part of the country through winters where the sun does not come up for five months.

Always changing and always the same. This is Finland.

A snowy road doesn't stop people from bicycling in Finland. Some bikes are outfitted with extra-wide tires to give them more traction in the snow.

CHAPTER 2

Cold and Bright

FINLAND IS A LAND OF EXTREMES. IT IS ONE OF THE northernmost countries in the world, with one-third of its area above the Arctic Circle. As you would expect, Finland is snowy and icy for much of the year. But it is also a place that comes alive with sunlight and growth for another half of the year. It is a place of rock and ice, of water and forests, of lakes jumping with fish and fields covered in wild-flowers. It has regions where the sun never rises in winter and never sets in summer. It is a place that is wild and unique.

The Lay of the Land

Finland is a relatively small country, about the size of the U.S. state of Montana. It is long and skinny, measuring 717 miles (1,154 kilometers) from north to south and 336 miles (541 km) from east to west. To the north of Finland is Norway.

Opposite: **Snow covers the trees in northern Finland.**

A man moors his boat along an island off the coast of Finland. With its long coastline and many lakes, Finland is a popular place for boating.

Sweden lies to the northwest and Russia to the east. The Baltic Sea serves as its southwestern and southern border. The arm of the Baltic bordering the west of Finland is called the Gulf of Bothnia, while that to the south is the Gulf of Finland.

Beneath the Surface

Finland is one of the few countries in the world that is actually growing! It is estimated that Finland gains about 2 square miles (5 square kilometers) of land every year. This happens because Finland is still recovering from the last Ice Age, which ended about ten thousand years ago. The glacier that once covered Finland was almost 2 miles (3 km) thick, and its weight pressed down and compressed the earth beneath it. When the ice melted, the land slowly began to bounce back. And that is still going on today.

Some of the earth's oldest bedrock—more than three billion years old—lies under Finland. There actually isn't very

Finland's Geographic Features

Area: 130,559 square miles (338,146 sq km)

Highest Elevation: Mount Halti, 4,357 feet (1,328 m) above sea level

Lowest Elevation: Sea level along the coast

Longest River: Kemi River, 340 miles (547 km)

Largest Lake: Lake Saimaa, 443 square miles (1,147 sq km)

Largest Island: Åland, 266 square miles (689 sq km)

Coldest Recorded Temperature: Kittilä, Lapland, –61°F (–51.5°C)

Warmest Recorded Temperature: Liperi, Karelia, 99°F (37°C)

Northernmost Point: Nuorgam, Lapland

Southernmost Point: Bogskär, Åland region

Polluted waters in the Baltic Sea. In recent years, Finland has eliminated much of the pollution entering the Baltic.

Saving the Baltic Sea

Much of Finland's coastline lies on the Baltic Sea. The Baltic is a brackish sea, meaning that it's a mix of salt water from the Atlantic Ocean and fresh water from rivers that drain into it. More than five million Finns (almost the country's entire population) live in the vicinity of the Baltic. About eighty million people in Denmark, Estonia, Germany, Latvia, Lithuania, Poland, Russia, and Sweden do as well. The good part about this is that millions of people get to enjoy the sea for recreation. The bad part is that pollution from millions of homes, businesses, ships, and farms ends up in the sea.

The pollution results in lowered levels of oxygen in the Baltic, and over the past century,

the health of the Baltic has declined. The pollution has caused declining populations of fish and other sea life, and giant areas on the seafloor where nothing can live at all.

Concern for the future has led all the countries bordering the Baltic to band together to try to save the sea. In 1974, the Helsinki Commission (HELCOM) was set up to oversee environmental protection of the Baltic. Thanks to international cooperation, the amount of pollutants entering the Baltic has been greatly reduced. The Finnish government in particular has worked hard to clean up the part of the Baltic that borders Finland, and only one of nation's main sources of Baltic pollution remains active.

much soil in Finland, and where it exists it isn't very deep. Rock, though, is plentiful. Granite and limestone quarries in the middle of Finland are very productive. Copper and zinc found in the rocks are also mined and sold internationally.

The Coastal Lowlands

Finland is divided into four regions: the coastal lowlands, the lake district, Lapland, and the coastal islands. Each has its own character, geography, geology, and climate.

The coastal lowlands, or coastal plain, varies from 40 to 80 miles (60 to 130 km) wide and stretches around the coast of Finland, from Sweden to Russia. The lowlands are flat, cut by many rivers that flow to the Baltic Sea. The climate in this region is the mildest in Finland, because of the southern location and because warm winds blow off the Baltic. Because of the region's more welcoming climate, most Finns live in the

Huge blocks of granite have been cut from this quarry in Finland.

Urban Landscapes

Helsinki, the capital of Finland, is its largest city, home to more than 600,000 people. Espoo is the second-largest city in Finland with a population of 266,000. People have lived in the area for about nine thousand years, but Espoo did not become an official city until 1972. Espoo is part of the Helsinki metropolitan area, but it has its own culture and economy. Many tech companies and startups are headquartered in Espoo, including cell phone giant Nokia, video game maker Rovio, and Neste Oil.

Tampere, in southern Finland, dates to 1779 when it was founded as a market town by King Gustav III of Sweden. Today, Tampere is a large city by Finnish standards, boasting a population of 223,000, making it the nation's third-largest city. As Finland grew, Tampere became a center of industry and it is still a hub

Old granaries in Oulu have been converted into shops and cafés.

for paper production and engineering. The city sits in between two large lakes, which provide plentiful opportunity for recreational activities.

Like Espoo, Vantaa, the nation's fourth-largest city with 211,000 residents, is near Helsinki. It is home to the main airport in the Helsinki area. The growing city is also home to the nation's major science museum, Heureka.

Oulu is sometimes considered the gateway to the north of Finland. This city of 197,000 is a magnet for people who enjoy the outdoors or art, or who work in modern high-tech. Oulu sits on the Bay of Bothnia and is surrounded by many parks. It has the largest network of bicycle paths in the country, and people use them even in winter. Oulu hosts Qstock, a two-day music festival every July, and the Air Guitar World Championship in August. It is also home to Rokua Geopark, where you can see landforms that date to the Ice Age.

The Tammerkoski River cuts through Tampere.

lowlands. The major cities of Helsinki, Espoo, and Turku are in this region, as is the best farmland in the country. Most of Finland's fifty thousand farms are located in the coastal lowlands. Finnish farmers mainly grow grains such as barley, oats, wheat, and rye.

The Lake District

The middle of Finland is known as the lake district, or Lakeland. There is good reason for this. Finland contains about 188,000 lakes, and most of them are in this region. About one-quarter of the center of Finland is covered in lakes. The district is just north of the coastal lowlands. The two regions are separated by the Salpausselkä ridges. These are terminal moraines—long ridges carved into the earth when a glacier passes by.

Some lakes in Finland are too tiny to sail a boat on. Others are enormous. The country's largest lake is Lake Saimaa,

Ice fishing is a popular pastime in Finland. First, a hole is cut in the ice on a frozen lake and then a fishing line is dropped through the hole into the water below.

Spruce trees bend under the weight of the snow.

which spreads across the land in the southeast. The lake is part of an important transportation route called the Saimaa Canal, which opened in 1856. Running for 27 miles (43 km), the canal links Lake Saimaa to Vyborg, Russia. Canal traffic includes freighters transporting goods between the countries, as well as pleasure boats carrying tourists and vacationers.

Lake Päijänne is the second-largest lake in Finland. It drains south into the Gulf of Finland via the Kymi River. Lake Päijänne is connected to the Finnish capital, Helsinki, by the Päijänne Water Tunnel. This is an underground aqueduct, or a system of pipes, that brings drinking water to Helsinki.

Many Finns own or rent vacation homes in the lake district. There are nearly a half million of these vacation cabins, called *mökkis*, in Finland. Most Finns visit one every year in search of restful solitude. In summer many families spend their vacations swimming and boating. In winter they can be found skating, sledding, and ice fishing on the lakes.

Lapland

The northernmost part of Finland, above the Arctic Circle, is called Lapland. This is what many people think of when they think of Finland. Winter lasts about seven months in Lapland, from late August until April. The region is dotted with spruce and pine trees and is often blanketed in a thick layer of snow. Lapland is known as the place where reindeer come from. It is also the home of the Sami people, whose ancestors have lived there for thousands of years. The Sami were traditionally hunters and reindeer herders, and some still engage in herding.

Lapland is the largest region in Finland. It is mostly made of high plateaus, lakes, and swampland. Finland's highest mountain, Mount Halti, is in Lapland. It is part of a small ridge of mountains that borders Sweden and Norway. The very northernmost part of Lapland is tundra, a region where the ground stays frozen all the time. Very little can grow in the tundra. Most plants do not have roots that can reach down through the frozen, rocky soil. The only living things in the tundra are mosses, lichen, and shrubs that have shallow roots and need little sunlight.

The sun never sets in Lapland in summertime, making it a popular vacation destination for people wanting to experience the midnight sun.

The Coastal Islands

Finland contains a huge number of islands, some 180,000 of them. Most of Finland's islands are located off the coast. Some are so tiny that they are too small for even one house. These are called skerries. The most famous Finnish islands are the Åland Islands, which lie in the Baltic between Sweden and Finland, off the coast of Turku. About 6,500 islands make up the Ålands, but people live on only about 60 of them.

Four Seasons

Perhaps nowhere on earth is the contrast between the seasons as extreme as in Finland. Winter is the longest season, beginning in November when the snow starts to fall. In some places, the snow doesn't begin to melt until April. Snow covers the ground all winter. Parts of Finland experience the polar night, or *kaamos*. For about fifty days a year in northern Finland, people don't see the sun. The southern part of the

The Åland Islands stretch out in a chain from the Gulf of Bothnia from southwestern Finland. About 90 percent of residents of the Ålands live on the largest island, Fasta Åland.

The northern lights are visible about two hundred nights a year in northern Finland.

The Northern Lights

The winter nights in Finland are long and dark. But without long, dark nights the aurora borealis, or "northern lights," would not be visible. The aurora borealis is a phenomenon caused by charged particles from the sun hitting earth's atmosphere. It looks like a colored glow in the sky—bursts of colored light. The aurora is often more visible the farther north you go on the planet, so Finland is a great place to see it from late August through April.

The Finnish word for the northern lights is *revontulet*, which means "fox fires." It comes from an ancient folktale about an arctic fox waving its tail and shooting snow up into the sky and starting fires. The Sami people of Lapland believed that the lights were the souls of people who have died. Traditionally, they were silent when witnessing the lights because making noise could anger the lights and bring bad luck or even death.

country gets brief sunlight throughout the winter. During the dead of winter in the southern capital city of Helsinki, the sun shines dimly for about six hours a day.

Temperatures in winter rarely get above freezing, but vary quite a bit from north to south. In Lapland, the temperature often falls below –20 degrees Fahrenheit (–29 degrees Celsius). The lakes in the center of the country may be frozen solid for five months. Sometimes even the Baltic Sea freezes.

Spring is short in Finland, lasting only as long as it takes the snow to melt. This usually starts in April in the south and creeps north by the end of May, when the temperatures rise to about 45°F (7°C). As soon as the snow and ice are gone, summer quickly begins with the sun brighter, days longer, and plants beginning to sprout.

Summer in Finland is fairly long, from about May to September. The days are warm, with temperatures anywhere from 50°F (10°C) to 95°F (35°C). During summer, Finland experiences the midnight sun, the opposite of the polar night. In northern regions, the sun never sets, while Helsinki gets about nineteen hours of daylight on the longest day of the year. The long summer days allow for rapid growth of crops and wildflowers, as well as lots of time for Finns to enjoy themselves outdoors.

A pine grosbeak feeds on berries in Finland. It is one of the many bird species that remain in Finland throughout the year.

The sun sits just above the horizon overnight during the time of the midnight sun.

Polar Night and Midnight Sun

The Arctic Circle cuts across northern Finland. The circle is an imaginary line around the earth that marks the southernmost point where the sun does not rise in winter for at least twenty-four hours in a row one day a year. The farther north you go, the longer the period of continuous darkness is. This period when the sun doesn't rise is called the polar night.

In the summer, the Arctic Circle marks the southernmost point where the sun does not set for at least twenty-four hours in a row. This is called the midnight sun.

These continuous periods of daylight and darkness occur because Earth is tilted on its axis as it orbits the Sun. It is summer when the part of Earth where you live is tilted toward the Sun and winter when it is titled away. But because of the tilt, the area above the Arctic Circle is always bathed in light at the height of summer, even as the Earth spins. On other parts of the globe, Earth's rotation produces the darkness of night.

Autumn is another short season. It begins in the north in late August and moves south within about a month. Plants stop growing by October and many animals go into hibernation before the snow starts to fall.

CHAPTER 3

Wild and Wooly

IF YOU LOOK AT FINLAND FROM ABOVE, YOU'LL SEE A country that's wild. About 75 percent of Finland is covered in forest, and 10 percent is water. Only 15 percent of the country is developed. Even in a city in Finland, you're never far from nature. Finns love to get outside. They hike, swim, and explore the natural world.

Finland is overflowing with living things, many of them unique to the country's unusual climate. The combination of cold, snowy winters and bright summers with lots of sunlight means plants and animals have to be strong and adaptable to survive.

Opposite: **Thick pine forests cover much of the land in Finland. About three-quarters of the land is forested.**

Plant Life

Thousands of species of plants grow in Finland. Many people think of evergreen trees when they think of Finland's wintry

In young silver birch trees, the white bark naturally peels off in thin, paperlike pieces.

climate. And Finland certainly has a lot of evergreens: Much of the country is covered in spruce and pine forest, even north of the Arctic Circle. But southern parts of the country have deciduous trees that lose their leaves. These include maples, aspens, and birches.

The silver birch, the national tree of Finland, is notable for its bright white bark. Although Finns use the tree for timber, it has many other uses as well. They use birch sap to make a drink, and birch bark has traditionally been made into things like shoes, roofs, and baskets.

Finland is also home to more than a thousand species of mosses and lichens, which are adapted to the harsh climate. Maybe most surprising is that in summertime Finland is covered in flowers. A thousand species of flowering plants can

People canoe down the Oulanka River near the Russian border.

Free to Be Outdoors

The right to be out in nature is one that Finns take seriously. There's even a law that guarantees it. Everyman's Right is a concept that says everyone in Finland, whether they are a citizen or a visitor, is entitled to roam any forest, field, lake, or pond that they wish, even if it is private property. Everyman's Right also allows people to collect any wild foods they find growing.

The idea behind this law is that Finns should be able to enjoy outdoor activities easily. But Everyman's Right comes with responsibilities.

People can only fish with a simple rod and reel. Hikers must stay out of private gardens and farms where crops grow. No motorized vehicles are allowed in open space. Before hunting or lighting a fire, visitors are supposed to ask the landowner's permission. And of course anyone who uses the land is expected to leave it the way they found it—littering and polluting are strictly forbidden. Everyman's Right makes it easy for Finns to take advantage of the natural treasures all around them.

be found in the meadows and mountains. Dozens of types of mushrooms and berries, including strawberries, lingonberries, and raspberries, also grow wild. Berry and mushroom picking are popular summer activities and are protected by a law

Species in Finland

For a small country, Finland is bursting with living things. In all, about 27,000 different kinds of animals, 4,500 different kinds of plants, and 7,500 kinds of fungi live here.

Type of Animal	Number of Species
Mammals	80
Birds	468
Insects	20,000
Fish	102
Amphibians	7
Reptiles	5

Wolverines are strong, fierce, and fearless.

called Everyman's Right, which allows every Finnish person to collect edible foods on both public and private land.

Animals

Finland is home to four mammals that are sometimes called the Big Four: the brown bear, the gray wolf, the Eurasian lynx, and the wolverine. These four mammals are considered fierce hunters, and in the past that reputation led to them being feared and hunted. More recently, however, the people of Finland have become committed to conservation, and the populations of all four of the big predators are increasing. Finns remain committed to making sure these animals survive.

The most common mammal associated with Finland is the reindeer. Finland is home to two types of reindeer. The Finnish forest reindeer is a wild deer found in eastern Finland and Russia. The northern reindeer is a species that

The National Flower

In the late twentieth century, Finns selected the lily of the valley to be their national flower. This small, white, bell-shaped flower grows wild throughout Finland. Though all parts of the plant are poisonous, the flower is beloved, so much so that the Finnish name for the plant, *kielo*, is also a popular girl's name in Finland.

After the beautiful bell-shaped flowers on the lily of the valley die, the plant produces red berries.

The brown bear is the national animal of Finland.

The Wildest Places: Finland's National Parks

Forty national parks are scattered across Finland. Each was created to showcase something unique about Finland's natural features and to create protected areas to preserve the plants and animals that live there.

Well-loved parks include Pyhä-Luosto, in Lapland. Here, visitors can ski, snowshoe, and see the northern lights in winter. They can hike in summer to see places sacred to the Sami people who traditionally lived in the area.

Oulanka is one of Finland's most popular national parks. Located in eastern Finland near the Russian border, it is a great place for hiking, kayaking, and canoeing.

Nuuksio National Park is only forty-five minutes from Helsinki. It is an easy place to reach when you want to get away from the city for a quick hike or kayak trip.

was domesticated by the Sami people of Lapland more than a thousand years ago. The Sami continue to herd reindeer, though the deer are often left to roam freely.

Plenty of smaller animals also live in Finland. Mammals such as the arctic fox and the red fox, the European mink, and the Siberian flying squirrel are well known.

Wild reindeer race across the snow in Lapland.

The National Fish

Perch is the most common fish species in Finland, so it is not surprising that it is the national fish. The European perch is greenish in color, with dark stripes and red fins. Perch usually live in ponds, lakes, and calm rivers, but they also live along the coast in the slightly salty water of the Baltic Sea. Perch are predators, gobbling up fish and other small creatures. They are among the most popular catch for Finnish fishers.

Perch are considered very easy to catch because they eagerly go after worms tied to the end of a fishing line.

Finland is also home to reptiles and amphibians, which have to hibernate through the cold winters. One interesting reptile is the viviparous lizard, the most northern-dwelling lizard in the world. The viviparous lizard is unique because it

A great gray owl flies low over the snow in Finland to hunt. These large owls have excellent hearing, making them able to locate prey tunneling 2 feet (60 centimeters) beneath the snow.

The Whooper Returns

Finland's national bird is a pure white swan called the whooper swan. It is a large bird, with a wingspan up to 9 feet (2.7 m). The whooper almost disappeared from Finland in the 1950s. It became a symbol of conservation, and more than six thousand of the birds now live in Finland. The majestic bird appears on Finland's one-euro coin.

Whooper swans are named for their loud, honking call.

gives birth to live young and does not lay eggs like most lizards do. This is an adaptation to the cold climate in Finland. If the lizard laid eggs, they likely would not survive in the cold.

Birds

If you really want to see spectacular wildlife in Finland, look up. There are over 450 species of birds in this small country. Finland's long coastline and position near the Arctic Circle make it home to many bird species that are rare everywhere else in the world. Finland's location also makes it a common stopover site for many bird species during their migration.

As a result, the country is a hotspot for bird-watchers. Every year, people come from all over the world to try to spot birds like the red-flanked bluetail, the Siberian jay, and the rustic bunting. Finland is also home to an astounding number of birds of prey, including more than ten species of owl, nine kinds of falcon, and over twenty types of kites and hawks.

CHAPTER 4

The Story of Finland

EARLY HUNTERS LIVED IN WHAT IS NOW FINLAND AS long as one hundred thousand years ago. However, the first people we have record of in Finland moved there around 8500 BCE, as the glaciers from the last Ice Age melted. For thousands of years, groups of hunters and fishers, including the Finns, the Tavastians, and the Karelians, inhabited the land. They probably interacted with one another. They also had contact with people from today's Estonia and Sweden.

By the eleventh century, Sweden—to Finland's west—and the Republic of Novgorod, part of what is now Russia—to the east—began to compete for power in Finland. Sweden sent Roman Catholic missionaries to Finland to spread the religion. Novgorod sent missionaries from its Orthodox Church. This was the start of almost three centuries of tension between the two countries. In 1323, Sweden and Novgorod signed the

Opposite: **Olavinlinna is a castle that was built in the 1400s in what is now southeastern Finland. It is the most northerly stone fortress in the world that is still standing.**

Sweden

Novgorod

Boundary established by the
Treaty of Nöteborg, 1323

Present-day Finland

Turku

Treaty of Nöteborg, which divided Finland between them. Sweden had control over what are now western and southern Finland, while Novgorod got the east.

Österland

Swedish officials worked hard to convince people to move to Finland. They gave away land and money to make it easier for Swedes to live in the new territory, which they called Österland, or "land to the east." As a result, life in Finland in the Middle Ages looked very Swedish.

The Swedes treated the Finns well in some ways. They were not considered conquered people, and they had representatives in government.

In 1389, Sweden, and Finland with it, became part of the Kingdom of Denmark. For more than one hundred years, clashes broke out as Sweden tried to break away from Denmark. Finally, in 1523, under Swedish king Gustav Vasa, Sweden-Finland broke away from Denmark.

Such warfare continued for most of Sweden's rule in Finland. Sweden was a strong power in the region, but it was frequently challenged by its neighbors. As Swedish citizens, Finns were expected to fight for the Swedish king, but they were not given much in return. For several hundred years,

Swedish Empire, 1660
Present-day Finland

SWEDISH EMPIRE

Trondheim

Jämtland

Karelia

Finland

SWEDEN
Stockholm

Ingria

Estonia

Livonia

Skåne

Bremen

West Pomerania

Swedish nobles were given more and more land in Finland. Finns were forced to lease the land back from the Swedes in order to farm.

The Protestant Reformation

In the Middle Ages, the Catholic Church was very powerful throughout Europe. Church leaders had a lot of influence over the continent's rulers. But in the 1500s, many people

Turku Castle

For about six hundred years, the city of Turku, in the southwest, was the center of culture and trade in Finland. Turku is the oldest city in Finland, founded in 1229. It was planned as a marketplace and trading post and quickly grew to be Finland's most important city.

Around 1280, the Swedish governor of Finland began building a fortress in Turku. He designed heavily fortified walls with towers at both ends and a house in the middle for himself. For hundreds of years, the castle continued to be expanded until it included more than forty rooms, including a banquet hall, a shooting gallery, and quarters for the king and queen when they visited from Sweden.

Turku Castle withstood six sieges and many battles over the years. In 1614, a fire all but destroyed the castle, and by 1814 it was in ruins. The castle was partially destroyed during World War II. It has since been restored and is now a place where tourists go to glimpse what life was like in medieval Finland.

in Europe started to question the Church's teachings and power. These people who questioned the Church were called Protestants, and their movement was called the Reformation. In the mid-1500s, the Bishop of Turku, Mikael Agricola,

A statue of Mikael Agricola in Turku. In 1536, Agricola went to Germany to study under Martin Luther. He then brought Luther's ideas back to Finland.

brought the Reformation to Finland. He embraced the teachings of a German named Martin Luther, whose ideas were spreading across Europe. One of Luther's ideas was that people should worship in their own language rather than in Latin, the language of the Catholic Church. Agricola translated the New Testament of the Bible into Finnish.

Russian Rule

Sweden's power in the world declined into the 1700s. Between 1700 and 1721, Sweden fought the long and bloody Great Northern War against Russia, Poland, and Denmark. Sweden lost the war and gave up land in southern and eastern Finland to Russia. For nearly another century, small battles regularly broke out between Sweden and Russia over Finnish territory.

Barges are anchored on the Saimaa Canal, which was constructed over the course of eleven years in the nineteenth century. The canal was widened in the 1960s.

In 1808, Czar Alexander I of Russia invaded Finland, intending to take it from Sweden. He succeeded, and in 1809 Finland under Russian rule was renamed the Grand Duchy of Finland. The ruler was the Russian czar, who was called Grand Duke. Russia did not force the people of the Grand Duchy to become Russian. The Grand Duchy remained an independent state, with its own senate. There was a Finnish secretary of state, who went straight to the czar with issues. Finns were allowed to keep Swedish as their official language, and they remained part of the Lutheran Church rather than joining the

Russian Orthodox Church.

Because Russia did not interfere with matters in the Grand Duchy, the time of Russian rule was peaceful. The czars encouraged Finns to make their nation stronger, and many Finns were loyal to the Russian Empire. In 1812, the capital moved from Turku to Helsinki because the Russians felt Turku was too close to Sweden. At the same time, Russia improved and expanded the city. For the first time in centuries, the Finns were not fighting a war. This gave them time to start to build industries and a stronger economy. The Saimaa Canal opened in 1856, providing a way for people to move goods through the interior of Finland. Railroads were built, and Finns began to excel at shipbuilding and papermaking.

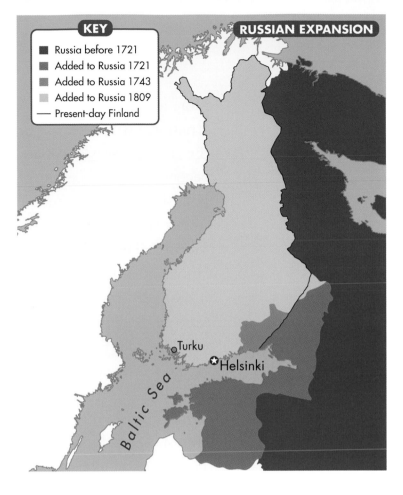

The Rise of Finnish Nationalism

The peaceful, prosperous years of Russian rule gave the citizens of the Grand Duchy time to think about the fact that they were Finns. They had been controlled by Sweden and Russia for hundreds of years, but they kept their Finnish culture.

More and more, they just wanted to be Finnish. In Helsinki, a nationalist movement began to grow. People started using the slogan, "Swedes we are no longer, Russians we can never become, so let us be Finns!" There was a new interest in the Finnish language. A man named Elias Lönnrot collected old stories and songs and combined them into a book called the *Kalevala*. This epic story was critical in the development of Finnish identity and the rise of Finnish nationalism.

Russian czar Alexander II was a liberal ruler and tried to support the Finns. In 1863, he issued the Language Decree, which made Finnish the second official language of the Grand Duchy, along with Swedish. This allowed books to be published in Finnish, and more and more people began to formally study the language. Alexander II also allowed the Finnish Diet, the main legislative body of Finland, to meet. This allowed Finns to make their own laws. The Conscription Act of 1878 gave Finland an army of its own. Though still under Russian rule, the Finnish nation was becoming stronger.

Russification: The Era of Oppression

The friendly climate for Finns did not last long. In 1894 a new czar, Nicholas II, rose to power in Russia. He almost immediately began stripping away the freedoms the Finns had gained. He took away Finnish self-rule with the February Manifesto of 1899. In 1900, he issued the Language Manifesto, which made Russian the official language of Finland. He ended the Finns' right to free speech. In 1901, he abolished Finland's army and made all Finnish soldiers part of the Russian army.

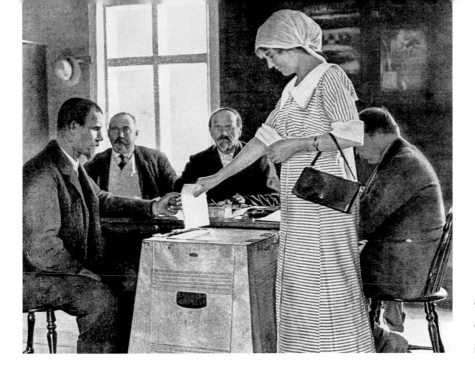

The Finns rebelled almost immediately using a method called passive resistance. They did not fight, but rather did things like going on strike and refusing to work. Children refused to learn Russian in school. People signed petitions against the czar. None of these things made a difference, however. By 1904, Finns started actively fighting Russian rule. On June 6, 1904, a Finn assassinated the Russian governor-general as an act of protest.

Russia was also facing trouble in other parts of the world. In early 1904, Russia lost a war against Japan. At home, Russian revolutionaries were making trouble for the czar with strikes and protests. All of this gave hope to the Finnish nationalists, who continued to pressure Russia for more freedoms.

Finns also pressured the czar to expand the right to vote and to form a parliament. Women's organizations were central to this effort. In 1906, the czar gave in to the pressure and allowed Finns to form a parliament with elected representatives. Prior to these changes, only about 10 percent of men and no women were allowed to vote. Now, all Finns, including women, were given the right to vote. This made Finland the first country in Europe and the second in the world to allow women voting rights. Many women also ran for office. Ten percent of the representatives in the first Finnish Parliament were women.

Even though Finland now had its own parliament, Finns didn't gain any real independence. The czar allowed Finns to pass their own laws, but he refused to approve them.

In 1914, Russia entered World War I. There was no fighting in Finland, but Finns felt the impact of being part of Russia while at war. There were severe food shortages and trade all but ended. Finland's economy and people suffered, and the Finns' desire for freedom intensified.

Independence

The period during and after World War I was rocky in Russia. A group called the Bolsheviks overthrew the czar in a revolution. The Bolsheviks believed in communism, a system in which the government controls the economy and all of the businesses. As part of their rule, the Bolsheviks declared that all people in Russian territories had the right to self-rule. On December 6, 1917, the Finnish Parliament approved the Declaration of Independence. Finland was free.

But freedom did not flow smoothly at first. In 1918, there was a civil war in Finland. The "Reds," mostly workers and peasants who were supported by Bolshevik Russia, fought the "Whites," wealthy landowners backed by Germany. The war lasted only a few months, but tens of thousands of Finns died. The bad feelings between people on both sides lasted a long time.

When the war ended, Finns faced the question of forming a new government. Some wanted a monarchy. They proposed making the commander of the White army, Carl Gustaf Mannerheim, king. More Finns wanted their country to be a republic, headed by an elected president. Mannerheim ran against Kaarlo Juho Ståhlberg in the election in 1919 and lost. Ståhlberg became the first president of a modern, free Finland. He also wrote the country's first constitution.

Finnish White army troops march Red army prisoners of war through the city of Hanko, in southern Finland.

As commander in chief of the Finnish army, Carl Gustaf Mannerheim reviews troops in 1939.

National Hero

Carl Gustaf Mannerheim is one of Finland's greatest national heroes. Mannerheim was a politician and military commander who helped see Finland through its last days as a Russian territory and into its new life as a free country.

Mannerheim was born in Finland in 1867 when it was a Grand Duchy of Russia. He started his career as an officer in the Imperial Russian Army. He rose quickly through the ranks and became the leader of the czar's personal brigade. After the Russian Revolution, Mannerheim no longer felt comfortable as part of the Russian army because he was strongly anti-communist. After Finland declared its independence, he helped to organize a Finnish army and became its commander in chief.

Mannerheim led the White army through the Finnish civil war and then ran for president in the first Finnish election, but lost. Prior to World War II, he oversaw the building of the Mannerheim Line, a series of fortifications in Karelia, a region of eastern Finland. The fortifications were designed to protect Finland from invasion.

When Finland entered World War II, Mannerheim once again led the army. He became more popular than ever and was elected president of Finland in 1944. He died in 1951.

Today, Mannerheim's birthday, June 4, is celebrated as Flag Day in Finland and is Finnish Armed Forces Day, a day of military honors.

Tough Times and Good Times

The period following independence was hard in Finland. In 1918 and 1919, a flu epidemic killed millions of people all over the world. Finland was not spared. About twenty-five thousand Finns died in the epidemic. Food and medicine shortages were common.

Through it all, the Finnish people kept working to strengthen their new nation. The lumber industry grew every year. Agricultural production was successful. Finland's economy expanded, and Finns gained an international reputation for being good business partners.

After the tough times, the Finns turned their attention to social welfare. They believed that a nation had a responsibility

Logs that have been floated down a river are loaded onto a truck. The lumber industry was vital to the Finnish economy in the early twentieth century.

Finnish troops wearing gas masks ski across the frozen land during the Winter War.

to take care of all its people. With its economic success, the government built programs to provide for children, the elderly, and the poor.

World War II

During the 1930s, it became clear that Germany intended to conquer all of Europe. When Germany invaded Poland in 1939, Great Britain and France declared war. This was the start of World War II. During this period, Russia joined with neighboring countries to form a massive country called the Soviet Union.

In August 1939, the Soviet Union signed a nonaggression pact with Germany. The two countries agreed not to attack each other. At the same time, the Soviet Union invaded and seized Estonia, Latvia, and Lithuania, Finland's neighbors. The country then demanded that Finland give up territory near the Soviet border. Finland refused, and the Soviets invaded on November 30, 1939. This started the Winter War.

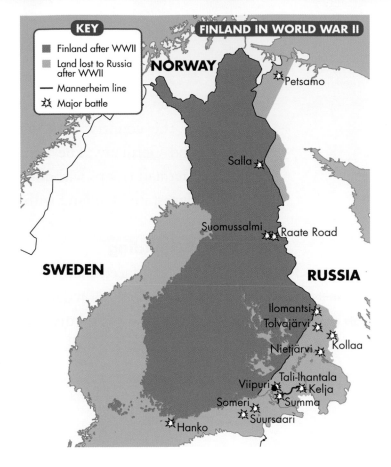

KEY

■ Finland after WWII
■ Land lost to Russia after WWII
— Mannerheim line
✰ Major battle

NORWAY

Petsamo

Salla

Suomussalmi

Raate Road

SWEDEN

RUSSIA

Ilomantsi

Tolvajärvi

Nietjärvi

Kollaa

Tali-Ihantala

Viipuri

Kelja

Someri

Summa

Suursaari

Hanko

The huge Soviet army overpowered the Finns. No other countries stepped in to aid Finland in the war, and it was over in four months. Seventy thousand Finns died or were wounded. In the peace treaty, Finland was forced to give up a large piece of Karelia, a historic region spanning the Finnish-Russian border, including the city of Viipuri. They also lost islands in the Gulf of Finland, a naval base, and land in northeastern Finland. About one-eighth of all Finns lived in these areas. They left their homes and moved to Finnish-controlled lands to escape Soviet rule in one of the largest mass migrations in history.

After the Winter War, Finns continued to fear the Soviets. In 1940, they asked Germany to help protect them. The Germans attacked the Soviet Union on June 22, 1941. In retaliation, the Soviet Union again attacked Finland. On June 25, Finland declared war on the Soviet Union in what is called the Continuation War.

Finland suffered during the Continuation War. One in ten Finnish soldiers died or was wounded. The war dragged on until Helsinki was attacked in 1944. It was clear the Soviets would win, so Finland asked for peace talks. The

Soviets demanded that Finland throw all German troops out of the country. This started another war, between Finland and Germany. The Lapland War of 1944–1945 ended with German troops withdrawing into Norway. As they went, they devastated Lapland with land mines and fires.

Rebuilding

Finns manufactured locomotive boilers as part of the reparations paid to the Soviet Union.

Finland faced many challenges as World War II ended. First, the Soviet Union demanded about $300 million worth of goods such as ships and machinery as war reparations. In order to pay this debt, Finland worked to industrialize and modernize its

industries. The work Finns had to do in order to pay the Soviets resulted in a strong economy and a robust export business that lasted for decades and made Finland into a modern nation. Finland's commitment to paying the debt also helped it form a strong relationship with the Soviet Union. Long after the debt was paid, the two nations remained close trading partners.

At the end of the war, Finland found itself with thousands of refugees who had fled Soviet-controlled areas and now had nowhere to live. The Land Act of 1945 called for the government to buy land and give it to refugees and soldiers who had served Finland in the war.

The Cold War

After World War II, tensions between the Soviet Union and the United States grew rapidly. The Soviets came to dominate Eastern Europe, and the United States was afraid that the Soviets would not stop there. Both countries feared the other would attack and both spent billions of dollars building their militaries. This period of competition and conflict between the United States and the Soviet Union was called the Cold War.

Finland found itself in the middle. The Finnish government wanted to keep good relations with the powerful Soviets right next door, yet it also wanted to remain free and democratic like the United States. Finland adopted an official policy of neutrality in the Cold War. On April 6, 1948, Finland and the Soviet Union signed the Treaty of Friendship, Cooperation, and Mutual Assistance in order to formalize their friendly relations. Some European nations criticized Finland for being

Soviet leader Leonid
Brezhnev (holding
flowers) visited Finland
in 1961. Finnish
president Urho Kaleva
Kekkonen, who served
from 1956 to 1982,
maintained friendly
relations with the
Soviet Union.

too friendly with the Soviets. But Finland used the treaty to its advantage, maintaining trade with the Soviet Union. In this way, Finland was able to stay free of Soviet influence at a time when other countries in Eastern Europe were absorbed by communism.

Peace and Prosperity

Finland continued to grow and prosper during the second half of the twentieth century, in part due to good relationships with both parties in the Cold War. The Finnish economy transformed from rural and agricultural to highly industrialized and modern. Finland thrived as it traded with both the Soviet Union and the West.

Finland's economic growth hit a bump in 1991 when the Soviet Union collapsed, and Finland lost a major trading partner. The economy suffered, and about 20 percent of Finns were unemployed. By the mid-1990s, however, the country's economy was growing again.

In 1995, Finland joined the European Union (EU), an economic and political organization of more than two dozen countries. EU countries share an economic policy, and trade within the EU is free and open. Some members of the EU, including Finland, share a currency, the euro. In the years since joining the EU, Finland has continued to grow and change with the times. Today, it enjoys good relations with all of its neighbors.

In recent years, the city of Espoo has boomed as a center for technology companies. In 2017, a new subway line opened to accommodate the growth.

CHAPTER 5

Free and Proud

I N 2017, FINLAND CELEBRATED ONE HUNDRED YEARS AS an independent republic. Finns are proud that their democracy has endured for a century, through the challenges of World War II, the Cold War, the formation of the European Union, and into a new millennium. They take their rights as citizens of a democracy seriously, and they express their opinions loudly—about 70 percent of Finns vote in each election.

In 1906, Finland became the first country in Europe to grant women the right to vote. At the same time, women also gained the right to run for seats in parliament. In 1907, the first time women could run for office, nineteen women were elected to the Finnish Parliament. Ever since, Finns have prided themselves on being leaders in gender equality in politics.

Opposite: **The Helsinki city band performs in Senate Square, the center of the city.**

Female First

Tarja Halonen, Finland's first female president, held office from 2000 to 2012. She was an extremely popular president, with approval ratings as high as 88 percent during her time in office, and only left the presidency because of term limits. Halonen was known for her focus on human rights. In 2009 *Forbes* magazine named her one of the 100 Most Powerful Women in the World.

Tarja Halonen began her career as a lawyer who worked in support of unions.

The Finnish national government is divided into three branches: executive, legislative, and judicial. But Finns are quick to remind one another that the real power of the government lies in the people who elect their leaders.

The Executive Branch

Finland's executive branch of government includes the president, the prime minister, and the cabinet, or Council of State. The president is the head of state, meaning he or she leads Finland's foreign relations and is the commander in chief of the military. Finnish presidents are elected for a term of six years, and cannot serve more than two terms.

The prime minister acts as the head of government. He or she is nominated by the president and elected by parliament. The prime minister appoints the heads of each cabinet department. These include Defense, Education and Culture, and Justice. These twelve ministers together make up the Council of State.

President and Peacemaker

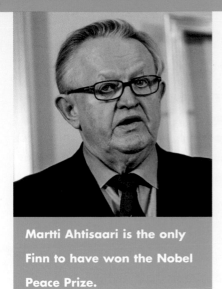

Martti Ahtisaari is the only Finn to have won the Nobel Peace Prize.

Martti Ahtisaari served as president of Finland from 1994 to 2000. Before becoming president, Ahtisaari was a diplomat, representing Finland in Tanzania and at the United Nations, where he was Deputy Secretary-General, Commissioner for Namibia, and Under-Secretary-General. In 2008 he was awarded the Nobel Peace Prize for his work resolving international conflicts in places like Namibia, Kosovo, Indonesia, and Iraq.

The Legislative Branch

Finland's parliament, the Eduskunta, has two hundred members who are elected by the people to four-year terms. They make laws, supervise the national budget, approve international relations, and supervise all activities of the government.

Seats in the parliament are awarded based on proportional representation. This means that the more votes a political party gets in an election, the more seats it gets in parliament. Finland has dozens of political parties. They have to work together in parliament since no one party represents a majority of the people.

The Judicial Branch

Finland's judicial branch consists of twenty-seven district courts, six courts of appeal, and a supreme court. The district courts hear criminal and civil cases and deal with matters like divorce and child custody.

There is no trial by jury in Finland. Some district cases

The Flag of Finland

The flag of Finland was adopted in 1918. It shows a blue cross on a white background. The blue represents the country's many lakes, and the white represents the thick snow that blankets the country in the winter.

The Finnish flag was adopted less than six months after Finland became independent.

Members of the Finnish Parliament gather for a vote.

are heard by a panel of judges. Finnish courts also sometimes use lay judges, people chosen from the community to act as additional judges in criminal cases. Lay judges are chosen to

represent the age, gender, and ethnic makeup of a community.

If a person disagrees with the decision in a district court, he or she can ask for a court of appeal to review it. In addition to hearing appeals, the six courts of appeal also try more serious crimes like treason or misconduct by elected officials.

The Supreme Court is located in Helsinki. It is made up of a president and eighteen justices. The supreme court hears appeals and rules on matters that affect the law of Finland.

The National Government of Finland

Executive Branch
President
Prime Minister
Council of State

Legislative Branch
Parliament
(200 members)

Judicial
Supreme Court
Courts of Appeal
District Courts

Regional and Local Government

Regional government in Finland is managed by six Regional State Administrative Agencies. The agencies oversee things

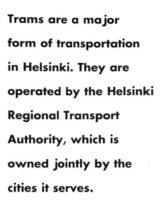

Trams are a major form of transportation in Helsinki. They are operated by the Helsinki Regional Transport Authority, which is owned jointly by the cities it serves.

like public services, education and cultural services, legal and civil rights, and environmental protection in each region.

Finland is divided into more than three hundred municipalities, or local governments. Each of these has a municipal council, whose members are elected every four years. The council represents the will of the people, so decisions typically reflect the opinions of the community. Municipal councils are responsible for all local services, including law enforcement, education, land use, health care, and economic development.

The European Union

Finland has been a member of the European Union (EU) since 1995. The EU is a political and economic organization of more than two dozen countries that works toward the common goals of peace, prosperity, and civil and human rights for all citizens. The EU has its own parliament, which passes laws, works on international agreements, and keeps the EU's budget.

The EU government also includes the European Council,

Helsinki: Capital City

Finland's capital, Helsinki, was founded in 1550 by King Gustav Vasa of Sweden as a center for trading on the Baltic Sea. Helsinki has been Finland's capital since 1812, when it replaced Turku in that role.

Today, Helsinki is home to about 624,000 people. Roughly 1.4 million people, more than one-quarter of all residents of Finland, live in the city and its suburbs. Most of them are ethnic Finns, but about 130,000 immigrants also call the city home. Most of Finland's major businesses are located in or near Helsinki. Like all of Finland, Helsinki has dark, cold winters. Summers warm up nicely with highs of around 70°F (21°C). At this time, lots of people are outside in cafés and parks, enjoying the long days.

Helsinki is located at the tip of a peninsula that extends into the Gulf of Finland.

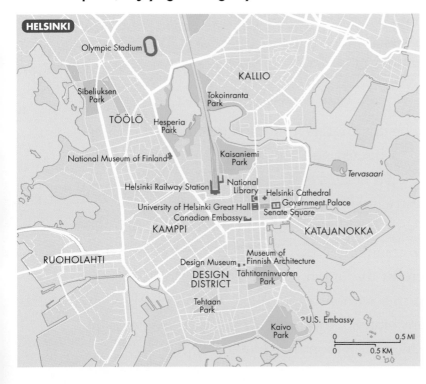

Helsinki is a beautiful city, known for its mix of old and new. The heart of the city is Senate Square, which contains four grand buildings: Helsinki Cathedral, the Government Palace, the University of Helsinki's main building, and the National Library. Nearby is the Design District, which includes the Museum of Finnish Architecture and the Design Museum. Helsinki is a world leader in design; many people come here to study and research as well as to shop.

Suomenlinna is the world's largest sea fortress. It sits on a chain of islands off the coast of Helsinki. Today, it is a military museum and nature area and one of the most popular attractions in Finland.

In 1952, Helsinki hosted the Summer Olympics. The stadium built for that event still stands and is used for sporting events and concerts.

*Note: The United Kingdom is scheduled to leave the European Union in March 2019.

EUROPEAN UNION

FINLAND
SWEDEN
ESTONIA
NETHERLANDS
LATVIA
DENMARK
LITHUANIA
IRELAND
UNITED KINGDOM*
POLAND
BELGIUM
GERMANY
LUXEMBOURG
CZECH REP.
SLOVAKIA
AUSTRIA
FRANCE
HUNGARY
SLOVENIA
ROMANIA
CROATIA
PORTUGAL
BULGARIA
SPAIN
ITALY
GREECE
MALTA
CYPRUS

KEY

■ EU member state
■ EU member state using the euro

which is made up of ministers from each member nation. The council meets to discuss and adopt laws and policies. The European Council is headed by a president. This office rotates, with each country holding the presidency for six months.

Belonging to the EU gives Finland the benefits of being part of a large community. EU citizens can travel and work freely anywhere in the union, companies can do business in other EU countries without restrictions, and people throughout Europe are granted the same rights and privileges no matter which member nation they live in.

Finland's National Anthem

Finland's national anthem is unusual because it has not been established by a law. Rather, "Maame" ("Our Land") is a national anthem because of tradition, adopted more than a century ago by virtue of its popularity among the Finnish people. The music was written by Fredrik Pacius, with lyrics (originally in Swedish) by Johan Ludvig Runeberg. The song was performed for the first time in 1848.

English translation

Oh our land, Finland, fatherland,
ring, golden word!
No valley, no hill,
no water, shore more dear
Than this northern homeland,
the dear land of our fathers

Your bloom will
bud from its shell for once;
Our love will raise
your hope, your joy in glory,
And for once your song, fatherland,
Will get a higher echo

CHAPTER 6

Small Nation, Big Economy

FINLAND MIGHT BE SMALL, BUT IT HAS ONE OF THE strongest economies in Europe. Just a hundred years ago, its economy was traditional. Most people worked in farming, fishing, or forestry. Today, Finland is a highly industrialized country. Many people are employed in manufacturing and industry, although forestry is still important. Changing with the times in order to stay successful is a Finnish value and it shows. Finland is also known as a place where innovation and change are encouraged, and many technology companies thrive here.

Opposite: **A Woman stands in front of a pile of logs outside a mill in Joensuu, in eastern Finland. The city was founded as a site for sawmills, and forestry remains important to the local economy.**

At Your Service

More Finns work in service industries than any other sector of the economy. Services include things like health care, design, education, and tourism.

Tourism is an especially important service industry in Finland. More than seven million people per year visit the country, bringing in about $3 billion to the Finnish economy. They come to enjoy everything from art in Helsinki to magnificent national parks to "Santa tours" in Lapland.

From Land and Sea

Agriculture plays only a small part in the Finnish economy, yet Finnish farmers produce enough to provide the people with their basic foods. Among the most important crops are grains such as barley, rye, and oats. Finnish farms also produce

Reindeers pull sleds carrying tourists across Lapland.

Media Consumers

Finns value news. This country of five million people publishes over two hundred daily or weekly newspapers and more than four thousand different magazines.

Finns also get information via four national TV stations and six national radio stations. In addition, there are dozens of cable channels available. Finland is at or near the top of ratings of countries in terms of freedom of the press.

vast amounts of potatoes. Finnish farmers also raise dairy cows, pigs, chickens, and reindeer.

Fishing has declined in importance in the Finnish economy, though commercial fishers still catch salmon, trout, whitefish, and more.

A small amount of mining also takes place in Finland. Miners unearth metals such as iron, nickel, zinc, chromite, and copper.

Made in Finland

Exports are a big part of the national economy, and manufacturing is responsible for many of the goods that are exported. Metals and machines make up the biggest chunk of manufactured and exported goods. Engineering has long been a Finnish strength and many companies make goods related to cell phone and computer technology.

Although fewer Finns make a living in the timber industry today than in the past, forest products remain an important part of the manufacturing economy. Wood products such as paper and plywood are made in Finland. The country is a leader in making machinery needed to process wood and paper. Wood processing has gone high-tech in the twenty-first century, and Finland produces computerized machinery that makes more paper with less waste than ever before.

Finland has been involved in chemical production since the 1600s, when it led the world in tar making. Today, Finland produces chemicals used in forestry, farming, cosmetics, plastics, water treatment, and automobile tires. The technology boom in Finland

KEY

- Forest
- Pasture
- Cultivated
- Tundra
- **Au** Gold
- **Cr** Chromite
- **Cu** Copper
- **Fe** Iron
- **Ni** Nickel
- Petroleum
- **P** Phosphate
- **Pb** Lead
- **Zn** Zinc

RESOURCES

NORWAY

SWEDEN

RUSSIA

Reindeer

Cu
Au

Timber

Cr   Fe

Oulu

Cu
Fe Pb Zn
Zn Oats

Barley

P
P
Cu

Timber

Cr
Cr Rye
Fe Dairy   Dairy
Tampere
Ni
Turku Vantaa
Espoo
Helsinki

has encouraged many new biotechnology companies to start up as well, and some of these are developing scientific and medical chemicals.

With so many miles of coastline, Finland is a natural fit for shipbuilding. Finns have built boats for hundreds of years, but after World War II the country become a leader in ship-building. Finnish shipyards are especially known for building icebreakers, which are used to clear out shipping lanes during the long, cold winters, and luxury cruise ships that sail all over the world. Finland's shipbuilding expertise is also used to make oil rigs and small pleasure boats.

An icebreaker ship clears a path through the frozen waters off Finland. Finland has more icebreakers than any other country except Russia.

Marimekko is known for its bright poppy pattern.

Fashion and Design

For a long time, Finland was a center of wool and cotton textile production. That has largely ended, but the country remains a force in the world of fashion and technical clothing. Marimekko is perhaps the most famous Finnish fashion company, known for its distinctive geometric fabrics used in clothing and linens. Luhta is a well-known clothing company that makes high-tech winter gear.

Finns are known for having an unusual design sense that combines beauty with functionality and comfort. This style is used in everything from everyday objects like scissors to high-tech goods like cell phones and computers. Graduates of the University of Art and Design in Helsinki are in high demand around the world.

A penguin named Tux is the mascot of Linux.

Linus Torvalds, Creator of Linux

Linus Torvalds was born in Helsinki in 1969. When Torvalds was eleven years old, he started programming in the language BASIC. It was hard to get software in Finland, so he started writing his own software while he was still in his teens. While he was a student at the University of Helsinki, he became interested in computer operating systems, which led him to develop Linux. It is a free operating system that anyone is permitted to use in any way they like. It was originally designed for personal computers, but it has grown in use since the 1990s and now is in cell phones, computers, cars, and even home appliances.

Torvalds graduated from the University of Helsinki with a master's degree in computer science in 1996 and moved to the United States shortly after. He continues to work for the Linux Foundation, where he focuses on improving Linux.

High-Tech Finland

The story of Finland's digital revolution begins with Nokia. This cell phone company started off making rubber for tires and shoes, reinvented itself once into a telephone and telegraph cable company, and then in 1982 took a chance making something called a "car phone"—what would become the world's first cell phone. Nokia's success started a digital revolution worldwide and gave Finland a new focus on high-tech businesses.

Today, Finland is known as a place where innovation happens. More than half a million young information technology professionals live in Finland, and that number is growing.

What Finland Grows, Makes, and Mines

Agriculture (2017)

Barley	1,400,000 metric tons
Oats	1,014,000 metric tons
Wheat	802,000 metric tons

Manufacturing (Export value, 2016)

Machinery	$12.4 billion
Paper products	$9.33 billion
Wood products	$2.85 billion

Mining

Gold	6,000 kilograms
Chromite	2.7 million tons
Copper	320,000 tons

Want to Play?

Did you know that some of the most famous video games in history were developed in Finland? Finns have been programming and designing games since the 1970s. Game creation combines two Finnish strengths: technology and design. Some of Finland's video game exports have gone on to be played by millions of people around the world.

- Alan Wake
- Angry Birds
- Bad Piggies
- Boom Beach
- Clash of Clans
- Clash Royale
- De Blob
- Quantum Break

Finland is home to more than 240 video game companies, including Rovio, maker of *Angry Birds*. The Linux operating system was created by Linus Torvalds, a Finnish software engineer. Finnish companies are exploring clean technology, digital health care, new kinds of mobile technology, and more.

It is not surprising that Helsinki has become known as

the start-up business capital of the world. The Finnish love of innovation and change, combined with the country's business-friendly attitude, has created an inviting atmosphere for people to start new companies doing original things. Slush, the largest start-up innovation event in the world, is held in Helsinki every winter. Investors and inventors come to Slush from all over the world to connect and start new technology businesses.

Visitors try out virtual reality goggles at a Slush event.

The bridges and windows shown on euros are fictional. They do not depict specific places.

Common Currency: The Euro

Before 2002, the Finnish monetary unit was the markka, also called the Finmark. Since 2002, Finns have used the euro (€), the common currency of the European Union. Each euro is divided into one hundred cents. The euro comes in coins worth 1, 2, 5, 10, 20, and 50 cents, as well as €1 and €2. Paper money comes in €5, €10, €20, €50, €100, €200, and €500 bills.

Euro coins have a "common side," which represents the EU as a whole. The common sides show maps that represent the whole of Europe. The other side of an EU coin is the "national side," which features a design of the member nation that

made the coin. Finland's euro coins show various Finnish symbols: The €1 coin features two flying whooper swans, the national bird. The €2 coin shows cloudberry flowers and leaves.

Euro banknotes are the same in every country. They show architectural details from different periods in European history, such as windows, gates, and bridges. The windows and gates symbolize the cooperation and openness of the EU. Bridges symbolize the relationships between the people of Europe and the rest of the world.

In 2018, 1 euro equaled about $1.23, and $1 was worth about 0.81 euros.

CHAPTER 7

Who Are the Finns?

THERE ARE ABOUT FIVE MILLION PEOPLE IN FINLAND, and most of them are Finns. Finns belong to the larger group of Scandinavian people, which also includes people from the Nordic countries of Norway, Denmark, Sweden, and Iceland.

Finland does not keep statistics on ethnic or racial makeup, but rather classifies people based on their first language. There are two official languages in Finland—Finnish and Swedish. Until the late 1800s, Swedish was the only official language, and it remains a strong influence in Finland. All schoolchildren take classes in either Finnish or Swedish, depending on what their first language is, but they eventually learn both languages. Swedish is used alongside Finnish in official publications, on television and radio, and on public signs. Today, about 90 percent of Finns speak Finnish as their first language.

Opposite: **Finnish families are typically small. Most families have one or two children.**

KEY

LANGUAGES

- Finnish
- Swedish and Finnish
- Sami

NORWAY

SWEDEN

RUSSIA

Five percent of Finns are Swedish speakers, and about two thousand still speak the traditional Sami language of Lapland.

The Finnish Language

The Finnish language, or Suomi, belongs to a group of languages called Finno-Ugric. It is closer to Estonian and Hungarian than it is to Scandinavian languages like Swedish or Norwegian.

Since it is not part of the Indo-European language family, Finnish is very different from English and languages like Spanish. For example, there are no words for gender; one word (*hän*) is used for both "he" and "she." Finnish also has no articles like "a" and "the" in English. Nouns in Finnish can have any of fifteen different endings. Finnish words tend to be long. They are easy to spell and pronounce, however, because each letter makes only one sound and there are no silent letters. Few people outside of Finland speak Finnish.

City Living

About 85 percent of Finland's population lives in or near a city. As a result, the population of Finland is tightly concentrated in the south of the country, where most of the cities

How Do You Say . . . ?

English	Finnish
Hello	*hei* (HIGH)
Good-bye	*nakemiin* (NAH-ke-meen)
Thank you	*kiitos* (KEE-tohs)
You're welcome	*ole hyvä* (OH-lay HUU-va)
Excuse me	*anteeksi* (AHN-tehk-see)
Yes	*kyllä* (KUUL-la)
No	*ei* (AY)
How are you?	*Mitä kuuluu?* (MEE-ta KOO-loo?)
Fine, thank you	*Kiitos, hyvää* (KEE-toss, HUU-vaa)
Nice to meet you	*Hauska tavata* (HOWS-kah TAH-vah-tah)
I can't speak Finnish	*En puhu suomea* (EN POO-hoo SOO-oh-meh-ah)
Do you speak English?	*Puhutko englantia?* (POO-hoot-koh EHNG-lahn-tee-ah?)

Pronouncing Finnish Words

Finnish words always have the stress on the first syllable. Some differences between Finnish and English are below:

Letter	Pronunciation
a	like the "u" in "cup"
ä	pronounced like "a" in "cat"
ää	like "a" in "bad"
ai	"eye" as in "line"
h	always hard "h," as in "head"; never silent
j	pronounced like "y" as in "yellow"
ng	soft, as in "singer"
ö	pronounced like "er" as in "number"
öö	stretch out the "ö" sound
öy	"oh"
r	always rolled

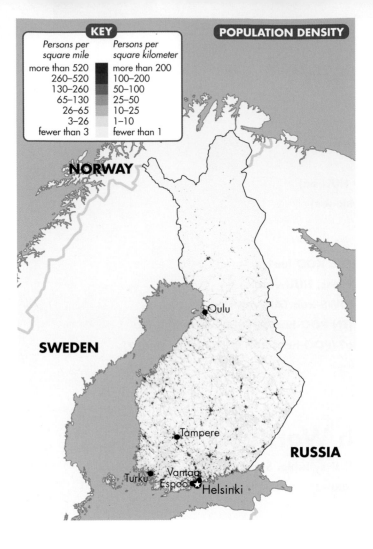

KEY

Persons per square mile		Persons per square kilometer
more than 520		more than 200
260–520		100–200
130–260		50–100
65–130		25–50
26–65		10–25
3–26		1–10
fewer than 3		fewer than 1

POPULATION DENSITY

NORWAY

SWEDEN

Oulu

RUSSIA

Tampere

Turku Vantaa
Espoo
Helsinki

Population of Major Cities (2016)	
Helsinki	624,000
Espoo	266,000
Tampere	223,000
Vantaa	211,000
Oulu	197,000
Turku	184,000

are. Although most Finns head to the country for vacations every year and many own country cottages, only 6 percent live year-round in rural areas. In earlier times, more people lived in rural areas. But after World War II, when Finland became more industrialized, people moved from rural areas to the cities.

Immigration

For a long time, Finland was not a place many immigrants moved to. In fact, for almost a hundred years, it was more common for people to leave Finland for places like the United States or Sweden than it was for people to move to Finland.

Like so much in Finland, though, that is changing. The friendly business climate and technology boom have attracted more foreign workers over the past several decades. At the same time, refugee crises in places like Iraq and Syria have brought many people to Finland. In 1980, fewer than fifteen thousand foreigners lived in Finland. In 2016, there were three hundred thousand.

Today, more immigrants are moving to Finland than there are Finns being born. In 2016, the number of Finnish and Swedish speakers went down by eight thousand, while the number of

people speaking foreign languages rose by twenty-four thousand. Immigrants account for about 5 percent of Finnish residents today. The largest groups of non-Finnish speakers are from Russia; Estonia; Arabic-speaking countries such as Iraq, Syria, and Afghanistan; and English-speaking countries.

Shoppers in front of a department store in Helsinki. More than a third of Finns live in the Helsinki area.

The Sami

The Sami are Finland's oldest ethnic group. They have lived in Lapland in the extreme north of Finland, along with parts of Sweden, Norway, and Russia, for at least four thousand years.

Finnish Somalis chat in Helsinki. Finland is home to about seventeen thousand people who speak the Somali language.

Traditionally, the Sami were hunter-gatherers. Their most important resource was reindeer. At first, the Sami hunted wild reindeer. Eventually, they became reindeer herders, and managed domestic herds for meat, milk, and transportation.

Today, about 7,500 Sami live in Finland. Most have typical modern lives and jobs. In fact, most Sami in Finland now live in Helsinki, but some remain in Lapland and maintain traditional reindeer herds to keep their cultural tradition alive. In 1996, the Sami Parliament was established to help protect the culture. The parliament has twenty-one members who meet to

The patterns used in traditional Sami clothing indicate which family a person is from.

National Minorities

Although Finland does not officially classify people based on ethnicity, the government has designated several groups as traditional minorities or national minorities. These are groups of people defined by an ethnicity or language who have lived in Finland for at least one hundred years.

Finland's national minorities are the Swedish-speaking Finns, the Sami people, the Roma (a nomadic group that lives throughout Europe), Jews, Tatars (Muslim Finns descended from Turks), Karelians (a group descended from traditional inhabitants of Finland), and Old Russians, people descended from Russian immigrants who came to Finland before World War II.

discuss cultural issues and protect the rights of Sami-speaking people. Sami are becoming more and more represented in Finnish culture: Children can attend Sami-language daycare; there is a daily news broadcast on Finnish television in Sami; and there are numerous Sami radio programs.

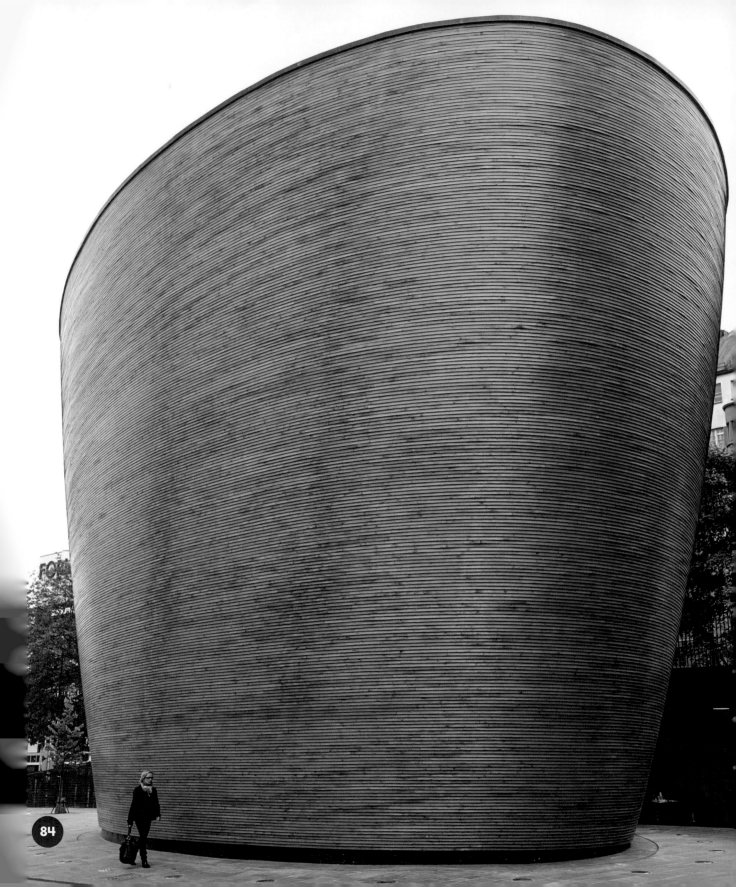

CHAPTER 8

Finns and Faith

Most Finns are Christians, and about 71 percent belong to the Evangelical Lutheran Church of Finland. One percent belongs to the Orthodox Church of Finland. Another 2 percent belong to other faiths, including Roman Catholicism, Judaism, Islam, and Buddhism. More than a quarter of Finns do not belong to any religion at all.

When a child is born in Finland, the parents agree on what religion the child will be. If the parents cannot agree, the mother makes the final choice.

Despite the official popularity of the Evangelical Lutheran Church, many Finns consider themselves culturally Christian but not religiously observant. Going to church is not common, except on major holidays. Only about 2 percent of Finnish Lutherans go to church weekly.

Opposite: **The Kamppi Chapel is located in a busy part of Helsinki. Known as the Chapel of Silence, it is a place for people to take a break and enjoy the stillness and quiet. It is not associated with any particular religion.**

A Syrian family on their way to Finland. Most Muslims in Finland are immigrants.

Religions in Finland (2017)	
Evangelical Lutheran	71%
Orthodox Church of Finland	1%
Other	2%
No religion	26%

Freedom of Religion

Though the majority of Finns still belong to the Evangelical Lutheran Church, the number of people choosing the faith is declining. Many see this as a result of Finland's strong policy on freedom of religion. The Freedom of Religion Act of 1923 gives Finns the right to belong to any religion they want—or no religion at all.

As part of this belief in religious freedom, Finnish children receive religious instruction in their own faith in public schools. Children who do not belong to a faith are taught ethics. Certain Christian customs, such as singing hymns at Christmas, are practiced in Finnish schools. These are considered part of a cultural tradition, and not a religious observance. Everyone participates, regardless of their faith.

Finland's Religious History

The early people who lived in what is now Finland were pagans, or nature worshippers. The history of modern Finland really begins with the rise of Christianity in Europe. Between the years 1100 and 1300, the Swedes brought Roman Catholicism to southwestern Finland. At the same time, Russians brought their Orthodox Church to eastern Finland. For hundreds of years these were the two main religions among Finns, with Catholicism being more common.

Many early churches in Finland were made of stone. The interior walls were painted white and sometimes covered with murals.

Helsinki's Uspenski Cathedral is the largest Orthodox church in western Europe. It was built in a Russian style, with a large dome surrounded by many smaller ones.

In the sixteenth century, Finland was under Swedish rule when the Swedish king Gustav Vasa joined the Protestant Reformation. He declared the Lutheran Church the official church of Finland. As the official church, the Lutheran Church had power over many aspects of government—including foreign relations—and education. In return, the government gave money and support to the Church.

The Finnish Orthodox Church has always been smaller than the Lutheran Church, but Finns have belonged to it for more than a thousand years. The Orthodox Church's presence in Finland reflects the history of Russian control over parts of the country.

The Evangelical Lutheran Church and the Finnish Orthodox Church remain the official religions of Finland.

Religious Holidays in Finland

January	Epiphany
March or April	Good Friday
	Easter Sunday
	Easter Monday
May	Ascension Thursday
	Whit Sunday
June	Midsummer/St. John's Day
November	All Saints' Day
December	Christmas Eve
	Christmas Day
	St. Stephen's Day

They are the only churches allowed to collect taxes from their members. They also receive money from the Finnish government. The money the churches collect goes toward church maintenance, social work, and maintaining graveyards.

Christmas and Easter

As an officially Christian country, Finland celebrates the main Christian holidays of Christmas and Easter. These celebrations look a little different than they do in other countries, however. Easter is celebrated in the typical religious way and, like in many countries, Finns use Easter to look forward to spring. Though they do this with bunnies and eggs, they also have an older tradition. In Finland, people decorate willow branches with feathers and crepe paper. Children dress up as Easter witches in bright clothes and go door to door with their willow branches, reciting a rhyme to keep away evil spirits, and expecting candy in return. The rhyme, "*Virvon, varvon, tuoreeks terveeks, tulevaks vuodeks; vitsa sulle, palkka mulle!*" translates to "I wave a twig for a fresh and healthy year ahead; a twig for you, a treat for me!" This practice combines a Russian Orthodox tradition that uses willow to represent the palms laid down in front of Jesus on Palm Sunday, and a Swedish tradition where children made fun of the fear that witches prowled around on Easter Sunday.

Christmas in Finland also looks traditionally Finnish. The celebration at home is on Christmas Eve. After dinner and

To dress as witches for Easter, Finnish children wear colorful clothes and paint freckles on their faces.

a sauna, Santa Claus visits and asks, "Are there any well-behaved children here?" When a family says yes, Santa leaves presents. Finnish families also sometimes make visits to the graves of family members who have died and light candles there on Christmas Eve. Christmas Day itself is a quiet day at home. The real parties with friends and family come on December 26, called St. Stephen's Day.

Cemeteries in Finland glow with candles on Christmas Eve.

Ancient Nature Worship

The roots of modern Finns' love of nature can be seen in the pagan religion of ancient Finland. The people who lived in what is now Finland, Estonia, and northern Russia followed a polytheistic faith, meaning it included many gods, based on different parts of nature.

Ilmatar, the spirit of the air, is one of the many gods in the ancient Finnish religion.

The main god was Ukko, the god of thunder and lightning, the sky, and the harvest. The Finnish word *ukkonen*, which means "thunderstorm," comes from Ukko. Ukko was similar to the Norse god Thor: They both were said to own a hammer or ax that they used to strike thunder from the sky. Ukko was married to Akka, the goddess of fertility and the earth. Other aspects of nature represented in the gods were water (Ahti, the god of water and fishing); trees (Tapio, the king of the forest); and the moon (Kuu, the moon goddess).

The early pagans also believed in spirits called *haltijas*, which were everywhere and could take the form of a human, an animal, or some other element of nature. Every village had a haltija, as did every family. Families would make offerings to the spirits to keep them happy and avoid bad luck. There were also haltijas throughout nature—in the air, the water, the trees. People often called on priests known as shamans to communicate with the spirits and ask them for favors such as a good harvest, a needed rain, or good health.

Hundreds of thousands of letters are sent to Joulupukki in Finland each year.

Joulupukki, the Finnish Santa Claus

The Finnish version of Santa Claus, Joulupukki, which means "Christmas goat," has deep roots in pagan traditions. Goats were once a symbol of fertility, and a goat was often sacrificed to the gods in the winter. Sometimes men would dress as goats and people would perform a ritual to symbolize rebirth.

This evolved into a myth where evil spirits wore goatskins (often colored red, and adorned with fur) to frighten children into giving them gifts. In the nineteenth century, around the time when Santa Claus was becoming popular elsewhere, Joulupukki's reputation changed, and he became a kinder character.

Today, Joulupukki is said to live in Lapland with his wife. According to the story, they don't live with elves, but with *tonttu*, pagan creatures that resemble garden gnomes. Joulupukki's sled is said to be pulled by reindeer that stay on the ground, unlike Santa's flying reindeer.

These ancient people believed that everything had a soul—people, animals, even rocks and trees. After death, these souls went to Tuonela, an afterlife that was underground or at the bottom of a lake or river. A shaman could go to

Sacred Animals

**Many animals closely associated with Finland today have been
important to the Finnish people since ancient times.**

Bears

Ancient Finns believed bears came from the sky and could come back to life after death. In a sacred ceremony, a bear was sacrificed for a feast. After the bear was killed, ancient Finns honored it by burying its bones and putting its skull high in a sacred tree. They believed that the bear could return to the sky and then come back to earth. The bear was considered so holy that people were forbidden to draw a bear or even to say "bear." Rather, people developed some code names for bears, such as *karhu*, which means "rough fur."

Birds

Ancient Finns believed that a bird created the world. Some people told a story of the world coming from a bird's egg. Another creation story says the earth was formed from mud scooped up in a bird's beak. The Karelians believed in a "soul-bird" called the Sielulintu. It brought the soul to a newborn baby and then came back to take the soul from that person after he or she died.

Tuonela and speak to the spirits and ask for favors or advice on behalf of the living.

Modern Paganism

Some people think pagan religions faded away long ago, but paganism is having a rebirth in Finland. Called Suomenusko, or "Finnish faith," this new version of an old religion is slowly gaining followers. It is estimated that a few thousand Finns participate in a modern interpretation of ancient paganism. They focus on nature worship, respect for Finnish tradition, and ancestor worship. Many of the old festivals are celebrated, including Juhannus, the midsummer festival, and Joulu, the midwinter festival. In 2013, a group called Karhun kansa (People of the Bear) became the first modern pagan group to register as a religious community in Finland.

CHAPTER 9

Finnish Culture

FINNS ARE KNOWN FOR BEING PRACTICAL, AND THIS IS reflected in their art. For a long time, Finland's contributions to art have been mainly in the fields of design and architecture—making buildings and objects that are useful and also beautiful.

Opposite: **Eero Saarinen was both an architect and a designer. His Tulip chair is a classic of modern design.**

Architecture and Design

Architecture has a long tradition in Finland. Many ancient churches are still standing, proof that Finns build things to last. But the nineteenth and twentieth centuries were when Finnish architecture really gained the world's attention. Perhaps the most famous Finnish architects of this time were Eliel and Eero Saarinen, a father and son who were born in Finland and moved to the United States. Eliel Saarinen was born in 1873. He first became famous for designing the

The most famous element
of the Helsinki Railway
Station is its huge,
stylized statues holding
globe-shaped lights.

Finnish pavilion at the World's Fair in Paris, France, in 1900, and the Helsinki Railway Station in 1904. In 1910, Saarinen's son, Eero, was born. The family moved to the United States when Eero was thirteen. Eero Saarinen is best remembered for designing the Gateway Arch in St. Louis, Missouri, and the wing-shaped TWA Airlines terminal at New York's JFK airport. He also worked in furniture design. His modern-looking Tulip chair is still in production today.

Another Finn who combined architecture and design was Alvar Aalto. His modernist design for the Finnish pavilion at the 1939 New York World's Fair was considered a work of genius. He also worked in furniture design and art. He is probably most famous for the Wave vase, a curvy glass vase that you can find in many homes in Finland and around the world.

Finland is one of the world's leaders in the design of beautiful, functional objects. In 2012, Helsinki was named World Design Capital in recognition of the Finns' excellence in this area. Many Finnish designs reflect the Finnish connection to nature. Finland is known for its wooden furniture with flowing lines. Also famous are bright, graphic-printed Marimekko textiles and Arabia pottery. In keeping with the Finns' focus on environmental sustainability, many design materials are local and objects are built to last a lifetime.

Alvar Aalto is famed for his vase inspired by waves. His name, Aalto, means "wave" in Finnish.

Literature

Finns are readers. In a recent ranking of the most literate nations in the world, Finland came in first. The study looked at things like how many libraries are in a country, how many people use them, and how many newspapers citizens read. It's no wonder Finns came out on top: About 80 percent of Finns are regular library users, checking out books at least once a month.

The government supports Finland's literary culture. It gives grants to writers to enable them to work. This policy seems to be effective: Finland publishes about 4,500 new books each year.

Customers browse at a bookstore in Helsinki.

Elias Lönnrot was a doctor who spent years traveling to remote villages. On these travels, he heard much traditional folk poetry, which encouraged his interest in Finnish folklore.

The *Kalevala*

If you talk about Finnish literature, you have to talk about the *Kalevala*, the national epic poem. The *Kalevala* brings together many traditional songs and folktales. All of the stories in the epic were collected by one man, Elias Lönnrot, as he traveled around Finland in 1835. He then put them together as one epic poem.

The poem takes place in Kalevala, meaning "land of heroes." Kalevala represents Finland. The main character is Väinämöinen, a hero who has magical powers. The poem tells of his adventures in his quest to find a wife. The *Kalevala* also shows the transition of Finland from paganism to Christianity. It begins with the traditional Finnish story of the creation of the world. The final poem tells of the end of Väinämöinen's reign and is parallel to the arrival of Christianity in Finland.

The *Kalevala* was written at a time when Finland was still a territory of Russia. Elias Lönnrot collected the stories both

The *Kalevala* is made up of fifty long poems.

so that they would not be lost and as a symbol for the Finnish people who were beginning to struggle for their freedom. It was the first work of literature to be published in Finnish and is still the best-known piece of Finnish literature all around the world. It has been translated into more than fifty languages.

Modern Finnish Literature

The first novel published in the Finnish language was *Seven Brothers*, written by Aleksis Kivi in 1870. It is still considered a classic in Finland. It tells the story of brothers who want to live a carefree life in the woods, but who feel pressure from their community to become civilized and good members of society. The book is still seen as a story about the nationalism

The National Museum displays artifacts from ancient times to the present.

The National Museum of Finland

If you want to get a good sense of what happened in Finland from ancient times to the present, the National Museum of Finland in Helsinki is the place to go. The museum tells the story of the Finns in art and objects. You'll find ancient objects from the very first inhabitants of Finland, medieval weapons and coins, and exhibits on the folk culture of the eighteenth and nineteenth centuries. The ceiling of the entrance to the museum is painted in frescoes showing scenes from the *Kalevala*. The building itself was designed in 1904 by architects Armas Lindgren, Herman Gesellius, and Eliel Saarinen. They created it to look like the castles and churches of medieval Finland to pay tribute to the country's history.

that was taking over Finland at the time it was written, and the conflicts between rural life and industrialization.

Another famous Finnish novel, *The Egyptian* by Mika Waltari, is about a man who becomes the personal doctor to an Egyptian leader. Published in 1945, *The Egyptian* has been translated into dozens of languages and was the only Finnish book to be made into a Hollywood movie. During the same

Moominmamma
and Moominpappa
were inspired by
Tove Jansson's own
adventurous parents.

era, in 1939, the Finnish writer Frans Eemil Sillanpää won the Nobel Prize in Literature for books including *Meek Heritage* and *The Maid Silja*.

The Moomins

Probably the most famous—and beloved—characters in Finnish literature come from a series of children's books. The Moomins were created by Tove Jansson. The books, first written in the 1940s, follow the hippo-like Moomin family (Moominmamma, Moominpappa, and their son, Moomintroll) in their adventures.

Today the Moomins are bigger than ever. Jansson's stories have been translated into more than thirty languages and the characters are known around the world. You can see them in cartoons, books, and films.

Finnish hard rock band Lordi won the Eurovision song contest, an annual international music competition for bands from all over Europe. This put Finnish heavy metal on the map and now Finnish metal bands are popular around the world.

Finland has become a center of the music festival scene. The long summer sunlight makes a great backdrop for dayslong outdoor festivals that feature every kind of music.

Sports

By many measures, Finns are the sportiest people in Europe. According to a European Commission survey in 2010, Finland tops the list for physical activity. More than 90 percent of adults and children in Finland play a sport or do some other

Cross-country skiing is one of the most popular sports in Finland. Most Finns learn to ski when they are young children.

A batter reaches for a ball during a pesäpallo match.

The National Sport

The national sport of Finland is *pesäpallo*, or "Finnish baseball." Pesäpallo is similar to American baseball. Players hit a ball with a bat and try to run around three bases to get home. Some ways it differs from baseball are that the ball is pitched straight up in the air at the batter, the bases are laid out in a zigzag pattern, and catching a ball in flight is not an out.

physical activity multiple times a week. This culture of fitness is promoted by the government. Finns are guaranteed physical activity as a basic cultural right in their constitution, and government money pays for many facilities and sports clubs. There are over thirty thousand sports facilities around the country—everything from bike paths to ice rinks, and from gyms to archery lanes. Many workplaces have gyms on site and encourage employees to exercise or play sports together.

Finnish children take physical education class at school, but about 90 percent of them also play in a sports club outside school. The most popular sports are soccer, hockey, floorball (like floor hockey), and gymnastics.

Paavo Nurmi leads a pack of runners in a race in 1928.

The Flying Finns

Finnish athletes who are very fast runners are sometimes called Flying Finns. The first Flying Finn was Hannes Kolehmainen, who won three gold medals in the 1912 Olympics. He started a decades-long tradition of Finns being the best runners in the world. Another famous Flying Finn was Paavo Nurmi, who won nine Olympic gold medals and three silver medals in the 1920s. He held the record for being the most successful Olympic athlete until 2008.

Winter sports are very popular in Finland. Almost all Finnish children learn to ice-skate, and hockey is a national obsession. Professional Finnish hockey players are in high demand around the world. Dozens of Finns play in the National Hockey League in the United States and Canada, including top scorers such as Mikko Rantanen.

Skiing is another national passion. There's even a ski vacation built into many school calendars so Finnish families can get outside with their skis every year. Because there are no mountains in Finland, most Finns cross-country ski. Those who want a thrill try ski jumping. There are hundreds of ski jumps throughout the country for public use.

CHAPTER 10

Living Like a Finn

FINNS DON'T LIKE TO BRAG ABOUT IT, BUT OTHER people will tell you life in Finland is pretty good. Although Finns pay among the highest taxes in the world—up to 40 percent of income can go to taxes—this money is spent on vital services that people say make life in Finland better for everyone. Finland is always at or near the top of every international list of quality of life and happiness. Finnish schools are known for being just about the best in the world. The country is rated the best place in the world to be a mother. Finns have a lot of personal and political freedom, and the crime rate across the country is low.

The Finnish Household

Most Finns live with close family, but the look of the Finnish family is changing. In 2005, the average Finnish family was

Opposite: **Children leap off a pier in the Åland Islands. Spending time relaxing in the woods and water is an important part of Finnish culture.**

A Finnish wedding party walks from a church to the reception.

Married in Finland

Though the number of Finns choosing to get married is decreasing, some traditions still hold for those who do marry.

When a couple gets engaged, they both get a simple gold band ring. Then only the bride gets a wedding ring. Most weddings take place in summer. Traditionally, brides wear a white dress and a gold crown. Finnish wedding receptions usually feature a meal and music, but guests also play games, sometimes silly ones like musical chairs.

Same-sex marriage was legalized in Finland in 2017. Finland also allows same-sex couples to adopt children.

Name Days

In addition to celebrating birthdays, Finns also celebrate name days. This tradition dates back to when people celebrated the feast day of the saint for whom they were named. Over time, the practice evolved so that it now includes non-saints' names. The University of Helsinki publishes a name day calendar every year, containing hundreds of names. For a name to make the list, at least five hundred people need to have had it in the past fifty years. Names that are no longer used are dropped from the list, and new popular names are added every year. Finns typically celebrate their name day with a cake, and maybe small presents.

a married couple with two children. By 2016, the average Finnish family was smaller. Today, there are more married couples without children than couples with children. And couples are opting to have fewer children.

About half of Finnish families today have only one child. And only about 5 percent of Finnish families have four or more children.

A Finnish father relaxes with his children.

Work-Life Balance

Finns work hard and they play hard. Balancing work and home life is important to them. Most Finns work a pretty typical workweek of 35 to 40 hours. But included in those days are a one- or two-hour lunch, often with colleagues. Finns value the opportunity to get away from their desks and have a good meal. The talk at lunch is often about business, but you won't find many Finns eating alone at their desks.

The Finnish maternity package comes in a box that often serves as the baby's first bed.

The Finnish Maternity Package

When a baby is born or adopted in Finland, the government gives a grant to the parents to help them get started with the new addition to their family. Parents can choose either a payment of about $170 or a maternity package that is worth much more. It is a box full of everything they need to take care of a baby. About 95 percent of Finns choose the maternity package. The grant is both a gift and a symbol of fairness and equality: Every baby gets the same start. A typical box contains:

- Snowsuit
- 3 sets of booties, socks, and mittens
- Sleep sack
- 6 bodysuits of different sizes
- 7 pairs of leggings and tights
- Wool cap, lightweight cap, and a snow hood
- 2 sets of overalls
- Mattress
- Mattress protector
- Blanket
- Duvet and cover
- Diaper holder
- Towel
- 2 bibs
- Personal care items (nail clippers, thermometer, hairbrush, toothbrush)
- Cuddly toy
- Book

Finns have a lot of vacation time. By law, they earn at least five weeks off per year. In addition, most businesses shut down for the whole month of July and employees are not required to work. With about two months off per year, Finns have plenty of time to spend with family, pursue hobbies, or just relax and get away from the stress of work.

Finland also supports families with children so that both parents can work. By law, every mother in Finland is entitled to about four months off at full pay when she has a baby or adopts a child. Fathers get about nine paid weeks off, and there is another leave of about six months that the two parents can divide up as they like. In all, this allows for new babies to be home with their parents for about a year. All Finnish parents get money from the government to be used toward childcare, and every child is guaranteed a spot at a local nursery or day-care. About 75 percent of both men and women in Finland work full-time.

Universal Health Care

Another service Finns get for their high taxes is health care. Every Finnish citizen receives health care free of charge or for very low fees. Through the national health system, Finns can see a doctor or dentist, get care in an emergency room, receive mental health services, or get home health care if needed. Pregnant mothers receive prenatal care and follow-up care after a baby is born. Specialist doctors, nursing-home care, rehabilitation, and even guide dogs or therapy animals are provided if needed.

Finns also have the ability to buy private health insurance if they want, which gives them more flexibility in choosing the doctors they can see and the hospitals they can use.

In Finland, it is traditional to place flowers on a coffin before it is covered with earth.

Funerals

It is traditional to have a church funeral when someone dies in Finland. Unlike in many other countries, this typically takes place several weeks after the person's death. This is partly tradition, and partly because it can sometimes take time for people to travel in the harsh Finnish weather. Mourners typically wear black and bring flowers. Most people in Finland are cremated after they die, due to a lack of space in cemeteries. After the church service, many families will have a small reception with food, where loved ones can remember the deceased.

A Lifetime of Learning

Year after year, Finland's educational system lands at the top of the list ranking the best school systems in the world. Finnish students routinely score among the highest worldwide on tests of reading, math, and science.

How do they do it? Finland's education system is unique in many ways. First, it gives access to free education to every Finn, from preschool through adulthood, so no one is ever left behind. Finnish children start mandatory preschool at age five or six. The year they turn seven, they start what is called comprehensive school, which is required until they turn sixteen.

Finnish students learn the same kinds of subjects that other students do—math, history, geography, literature, civics, science, music, art, and physical education, plus Finnish, Swedish, and English. And the school year is much like it is in other countries. Finns go to school about 190 days a year, split between two terms from fall to early summer. There is a weeklong vacation in the middle of each term.

In many ways, the similarities end there. The school day in Finland looks different from school in many countries. First, the length of the day varies depending on how old students are. Children in kindergarten and first grade attend school for only about half a day, and they get at least fifteen minutes of play for every forty-five minutes of lessons. The day gets longer as students get older, but play and free time are always a part of the school day. Homework is a small part of school in Finland; most students have little or none.

Classes in Finland are fairly small, averaging about twenty students.

Playground Fun: Crab Ball Tag

Finnish students get a lot of time to run around and play during the day. One popular, silly game for a group is called crab ball tag. One player is "tag" and the others are "crabs." The crabs move around on their hands and feet, bellies in the air (like crabs). The tag has a ball that he or she throws at the crabs. If a crab hits the ball back with his or her legs or head and it goes out of bounds, the tag must retrieve the ball and can only throw it back in from the spot where it went out. If a crab is hit with the ball between the waist and neck, he or she becomes the tag.

Students eat two hot meals per day at school, free of charge. And school-aged children receive their basic health care, like dental exams and vaccinations, at school.

Teachers are given the chance to teach the way they think is best. They make up their own kinds of tests and plan lessons based on the needs of their students. Teaching is a very respected profession in Finland and one of the toughest to get into. Only about 10 percent of applicants are accepted to teaching programs, which only take the very best students. All teachers are required to have at least a master's degree.

Once students complete comprehensive school, they have a choice. They can follow an academic track, leading to college, or they can follow a vocational track, leading to training in a trade. Students who choose the academic track go to three years of what is called secondary school. This is like 11th and 12th grades in the United States, and it prepares them for university. At the end of secondary school, students take the National Matriculation Exam, a combination graduation exam and college entrance exam. Entrance to Finnish universities is very competitive. Not everyone who passes the matriculation exam and applies gets a place at a university.

Students who choose a vocational program spend three to five years in vocational school. They learn basic academic subjects as well as a trade. When they graduate they are prepared to get a job in their chosen field.

Finns don't have to stop learning once they graduate. Finland has a national adult continuing education system that

Students work on computers in the Helsinki University Library. Higher education is free in Finland.

Most Finnish summer cottages are small and isolated, a place to enjoy the peace and quiet of nature.

many people take advantage of. Some Finns choose to learn new things for fun. Others decide to take up a new trade. If a Finn becomes unemployed and needs a new career, he or she can go back to school free of charge. Finns credit their education system for their strong economy, ability to keep up with the times, and high standard of living.

City Homes and Summer Cottages

It is common for Finns to own a home. About 60 percent live in houses they own. Homes are smaller compared to many of those in the United States, and apartment living is common in the major cities.

Come summer, most Finns relocate for at least a little while to a cottage in the country. Many families own a summer cottage, while others rent. Like Finnish city homes, the cottages are not large or fancy—sometimes they're just one or two rooms. But that doesn't matter. The point is to get away from the city, enjoy nature, and take advantage of the midnight sun. Cities are often very quiet in July as everyone has left for the country. Families also use their cottages on the weekends for skiing, hiking, berry picking, swimming, and just relaxing.

Sauna

In the United States, people occasionally enjoy a sauna at the gym or a spa, but in Finland the sauna is part of everyday life. There are over two million saunas in this country of five million people. Sauna means "steam bath," and that is exactly what it is—a wooden building or room where stones are heated until they are very hot. Water is then thrown on the

A man in a sauna pours water on hot rocks to create steam.

Eat Like a Finn

In honor of Finland's hundredth anniversary of independence in 2017, the government did a survey asking Finns to name a national food. The results give a snapshot of both traditional and modern foods that Finns love. The winner was rye bread, which has been baked in Finland for about two thousand years. Other foods that made the list:

- Pizza
- Pea soup
- *Mämmi*, an Easter dessert made of rye flour and orange zest

- Fish soup
- *Viili*, a fermented milk product a bit like yogurt
- Karelian pastry
- Bilberry pie

- Fried herring with mashed potatoes
- Karelian stew
- Salt-cured fish
- Liver casserole

hot stones to create steam in the room. The temperature gets to between 170°F and 200°F (75°C and 90°C). After sweating in a sauna, people sometimes hop in a shower or bath to wash off.

Sauna is a tradition that dates back about two thousand years in Finland. Until people had hot running water indoors, a sauna was the only warm place to get clean in the winter. Many older Finns will tell you they were born in a sauna—it was often the cleanest place for a woman to give birth!

Today, the ritual of the sauna is a well-known part of Finnish culture. Many homes and businesses have a sauna. Apartment buildings have saunas for residents to share. It is traditional to sauna naked; men only sauna with men and women with women. Families will sauna together, though. But it is normal to sauna with friends and even coworkers—you sit in the steam for a while and chat and then cool down by taking a shower. Often, in the countryside, people cool down in a lake after leaving the sauna.

Finnish Food

Finnish food is fairly simple. Although imported food is becoming more and more common, imports are expensive, so Finns tend to eat what is easily grown in their harsh climate.

Hearty rye bread is part of most meals in Finland.

The most important elements of the Finnish diet are bread, meat, fish, dairy products, and coffee. Bread is usually made of rye instead of wheat. Finns eat a lot of rye crispbread, which is crunchy and hard, as well as soft, fresh-baked rye bread. Finns

Finnish pancakes are sometimes dusted with powdered sugar.

Finnish Pancakes

Pannukakku, or Finnish pancakes, is a traditional Finnish breakfast, especially on weekends. It is usually served with jam or berries.

Ingredients:

4 tablespoons butter

4 eggs

¾ teaspoon salt

2½ cups milk

1 cup flour

¼ cup sugar

Directions:

Preheat the oven to 400°F. Put the butter in a 9×13 inch pan and place it in the oven until the butter is melted. Whisk together the eggs. Add the salt, milk, flour, and sugar to the eggs. Whisk them together. Pour the batter on top of the melted butter in the pan. Cook for 30 minutes or until the edges are golden brown. Enjoy!

also eat a lot of pork and beef. Meatballs, ground meat, and sausage are daily foods. Anything that Finns can catch in the water is popular to eat. This includes salmon, herring, perch, and whitefish. Finns like smoked fish as well. Finns drink a lot of milk, and they make many good cheeses. The Finns also drink more coffee than any other people in the world.

Vegetables and fruits are not centerpieces of the Finnish diet because the growing season is short and imported produce is expensive. The Finns do eat lots of potatoes, wild berries, and mushrooms, however, because they do not have to be imported.

Like almost everywhere, Finland has its share of fast-food places. These serve anything from coffee and pastries to pizza, burgers, kabobs, and fried chicken.

A typical breakfast in Finland almost always includes coffee along with porridge or muesli (like granola) and bread. Many Finns have their main meal at lunchtime. All children eat a hot lunch at school and many offices serve lunch to workers as well. This is a meal of meat or fish, more bread, vegetables or salad, and maybe dessert. In the evening at home, Finns eat a lighter meal, maybe some smoked fish and bread, or cheese and fruit.

Nature Holidays

Finns celebrate some holidays that are closely tied to their ancient history of pagan nature worship. May Day, called Vappu, is celebrated on May 1. This is probably the biggest party day in Finland, with a carnival-type atmosphere. People take to the streets with horns, noisemakers, and balloons. May

During the midsummer festival, people dance around a pole decorated with leaves.

Day marks the coming of spring after a long, dark winter, and is a traditional workers' holiday (like Labor Day) as well as a big celebration for students. Finnish students all wear their white graduation caps. The festivities start on the evening of April 30, with parties and concerts in all major Finnish cities.

Midsummer, or Juhannus (St. John's Day), is in close competition with Vappu for the biggest party in Finland. The holiday celebrates the longest day of the year (June 21), when the sun never sets in parts of Finland. In ancient times the holiday was called *Ukon juhla*, or "Ukko's celebration," for the pagan god of thunder and rain. People had celebrations in his honor in order to guarantee rain for a good harvest. The modern name Juhannus comes from St. John the Baptist, whose feast day falls at midsummer. The midsummer festival is when Finns really get back to nature. They tend to head for the country, where they take advantage of many hours of sunlight

National Holidays

January 1	New Year's Day
January 6	Epiphany
March or April	Good Friday
March or April	Easter Sunday/Easter Monday
May	Mother's Day
May	Ascension Thursday
June	Whit Sunday
June 21	Solstice/Midsummer
November 4	All Saints' Day
November	Father's Day
December 6	Independence Day
December 24	Christmas Eve
December 25	Christmas Day
December 26	Boxing Day/St. Stephen's Day

and have big parties. Bonfires and cookouts are common, as are concerts and dancing.

Uniquely Finnish

Near the top of the world sits Finland, with all that makes it unique. In the years since becoming independent, Finns have been through a lot and accomplished a lot. Through it all they've managed to remain themselves. They are equal parts outdoors and high-tech, traditional and modern. They are people who are typically quiet and private, yet excel in international business and the arts. Finns look out for one another while still retaining their individuality. They remember where they came from while always looking to the future. They are uniquely Finnish.

Timeline

Finnish History

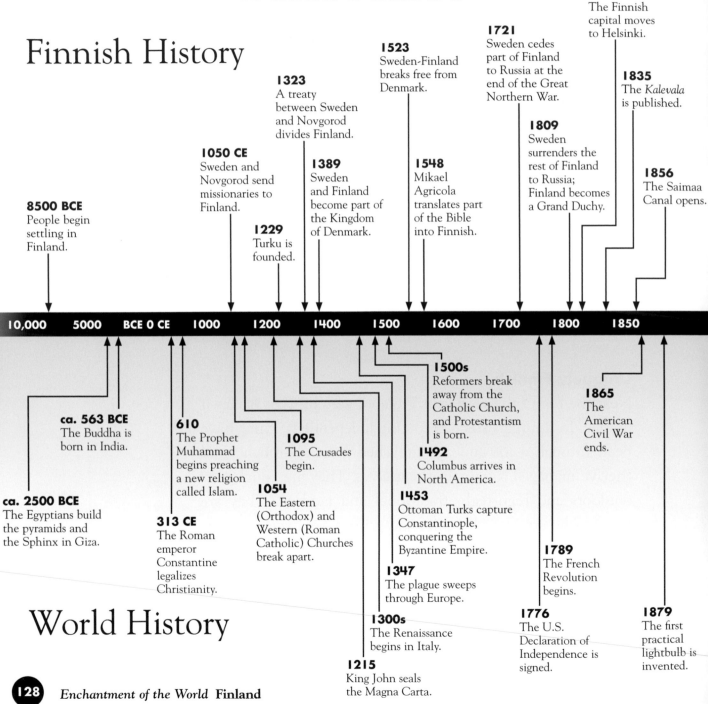

1812
The Finnish capital moves to Helsinki.

1523
Sweden-Finland breaks free from Denmark.

1323
A treaty between Sweden and Novgorod divides Finland.

1721
Sweden cedes part of Finland to Russia at the end of the Great Northern War.

1835
The *Kalevala* is published.

1050 CE
Sweden and Novgorod send missionaries to Finland.

1389
Sweden and Finland become part of the Kingdom of Denmark.

1548
Mikael Agricola translates part of the Bible into Finnish.

1809
Sweden surrenders the rest of Finland to Russia; Finland becomes a Grand Duchy.

1856
The Saimaa Canal opens.

8500 BCE
People begin settling in Finland.

1229
Turku is founded.

10,000	5000	BCE 0 CE	1000	1200	1400	1500	1600	1700	1800	1850

ca. 563 BCE
The Buddha is born in India.

610
The Prophet Muhammad begins preaching a new religion called Islam.

1095
The Crusades begin.

1500s
Reformers break away from the Catholic Church, and Protestantism is born.

1865
The American Civil War ends.

ca. 2500 BCE
The Egyptians build the pyramids and the Sphinx in Giza.

313 CE
The Roman emperor Constantine legalizes Christianity.

1054
The Eastern (Orthodox) and Western (Roman Catholic) Churches break apart.

1492
Columbus arrives in North America.

1453
Ottoman Turks capture Constantinople, conquering the Byzantine Empire.

1347
The plague sweeps through Europe.

1789
The French Revolution begins.

1300s
The Renaissance begins in Italy.

1776
The U.S. Declaration of Independence is signed.

1879
The first practical lightbulb is invented.

1215
King John seals the Magna Carta.

World History

1906
Finland becomes the first European country to allow women to vote.

1948
Finland and the Soviet Union sign a treaty of cooperation.

1917
Finland declares independence from Russia.

1900
Russian czar Nicholas II makes Russian the official language of Finland and abolishes the right to free speech in Finland.

1941–1944
The Soviet Union defeats Finland in the Continuation War.

1952
The Summer Olympics are held in Helsinki.

1995
Finland joins the European Union.

2017
Finland celebrates 100 years of independence.

1904
The Russian governor-general is assassinated by a Finn nationalist.

1945
The Land Act gives land to displaced Finns and returning soldiers.

Early 1990s
Finland's economy suffers after the Soviet Union collapses.

2000
Tarja Halonen is elected the first female president of Finland.

1939–1940
The Soviet Union defeats Finland in the Winter War.

2012
Helsinki is named World Design Capital.

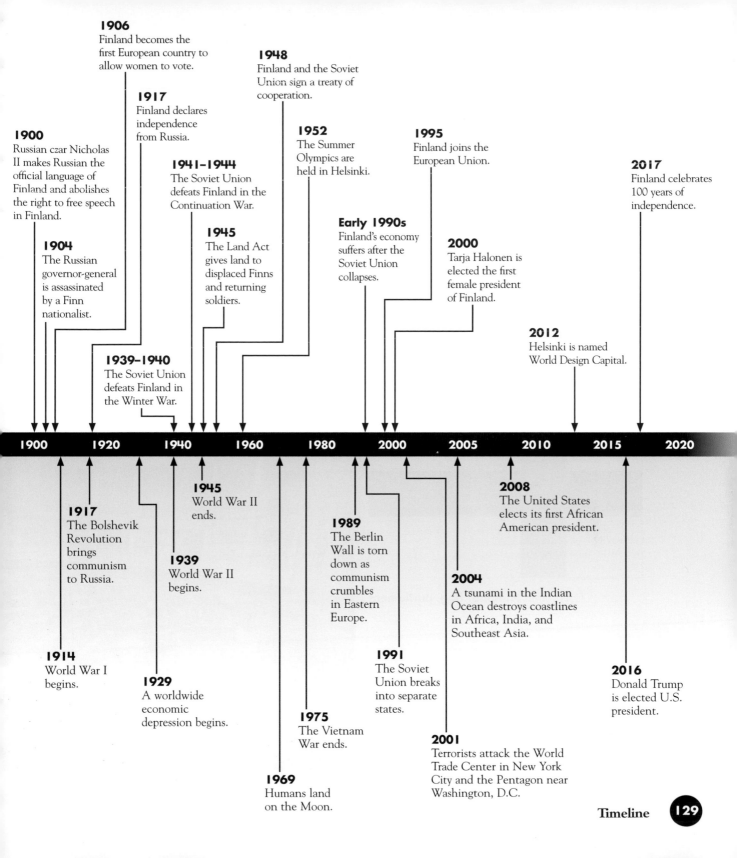

1900   **1920**   **1940**   **1960**   **1980**   **2000**   **2005**   **2010**   **2015**   **2020**

1917
The Bolshevik Revolution brings communism to Russia.

1945
World War II ends.

1989
The Berlin Wall is torn down as communism crumbles in Eastern Europe.

2008
The United States elects its first African American president.

1939
World War II begins.

1914
World War I begins.

1929
A worldwide economic depression begins.

1975
The Vietnam War ends.

1991
The Soviet Union breaks into separate states.

2004
A tsunami in the Indian Ocean destroys coastlines in Africa, India, and Southeast Asia.

2016
Donald Trump is elected U.S. president.

1969
Humans land on the Moon.

2001
Terrorists attack the World Trade Center in New York City and the Pentagon near Washington, D.C.

Fast Facts

Official name: Republic of Finland

Capital: Helsinki

Official languages: Finnish and Swedish

Official religions: Evangelical Lutheranism and Finnish Orthodox

National anthem: "Maame" ("Our Land")

Type of government: Multiparty republic

Head of state: President

Head of government: Prime minister

Left to right: **National flag, parliament**

Lakes and forests

Area:	130,559 square miles (338,146 sq km)	
Latitude and longitude:	61.9241°N, 25.7482°E	
Bordering countries:	Norway to the north; Russia to the east; and Sweden to the northwest	
Highest elevation:	Mount Halti, 4,357 feet (1,328 m) above sea level	
Lowest elevation:	Sea level along the coast	
Average temperatures:	**June**	**December**
Helsinki:	63°F (17°C)	21°F (–6°C)
Lapland:	55°F (13°C)	1°F (–17°C)
Average annual rainfall:	22.5 inches (57 cm)	

National population (2017 est.):	5,516,224	
Population of major cities (2016):	Helsinki	624,000
	Espoo	266,000
	Tampere	223,000
	Vantaa	211,000
	Oulu	197,000
	Turku	184,000

Landmarks:
- ▶ *Heureka*, Vantaa
- ▶ *National Museum of Finland*, Helsinki
- ▶ *Pyhä-Luosto National Park*, Lapland
- ▶ *Suomenlinna Fortress*, Helsinki
- ▶ *Turku Castle*, Turku

Economy: The largest sector of the Finnish economy is services. Manufacturing, primarily in wood, metals, engineering, and telecommunications, comes second. Forestry has traditionally also been a strong industry. Finland is a leader in telecommunications and design and in the early twenty-first century became a major hub for technology start-up companies. Grains and potatoes are major agricultural products, while important mining products include iron, chromite, and copper.

Currency: The euro. In 2018, 1 euro equaled about $1.23, and $1 was worth about 0.81 euros.

System of weights and measures: Metric system

Literacy rate: About 100%

Finnish words and phrases:

hei	Hello
nakemiin	Good-bye
kiitos	Thank you
ole hyvä	You're welcome
anteeksi	Excuse me
kyllä	Yes
ei	No

Prominent Finns:

Alvar Aalto *Architect and designer*	(1898–1976)
Mikael Agricola *Bishop and translator*	(1510–1557)
Tarja Halonen *President*	(1943–)
Tove Jansson *Writer*	(1914–2001)
Elias Lönnrot *Folklorist who created the* Kalevala	(1802–1884)
Carl Gustaf Mannerheim *Military commander and president*	(1867–1951)
Eliel Saarinen *Architect*	(1873–1950)
Jean Sibelius *Composer*	(1865–1957)
Linus Torvalds *Software engineer*	(1969–)

Clockwise from top: **Currency, Elias Lönnrot, school**

To Find Out More

Books

▶ Beach, Hugh. *A Year in Lapland: Guest of the Reindeer Herders.* Seattle: University of Washington Press, 2001.

▶ Bowman, James Cloyd and Margery Biano. *Tales from a Finnish Tupa.* Minneapolis: University of Minnesota Press, 2009.

▶ De Gerez, Toni. *Louhi, Witch of North Farm: A Story from Finland's Epic Poem,* The Kalevala. New York: Viking Kestrel, 1986.

▶ Jansson, Tove. *Moomin: The Complete Tove Jansson Comic Strip: Book One.* New York: Farrar, Straus and Giroux, 2006.

▶ Shepard, Aaron. *The Princess Mouse: A Tale of Finland.* New York: Atheneum Books for Young Readers, 2003.

Video

▶ *The Finland Phenomenon.* Bob Compton, 2011.

▶ *Moomins and the Comet Chase.* Maria Lindberg, 2016.

▶ *Seven Days: Finland.* Global Television/Arcadia Films, 2007.

▶ *Touring the World's Capital Cities: Helsinki—The Capital of Finland.* Peter O. Scarson, 2015.

▶ Visit this Scholastic website for more information on Finland:
www.factsfornow.scholastic.com
Enter the keyword **Finland**

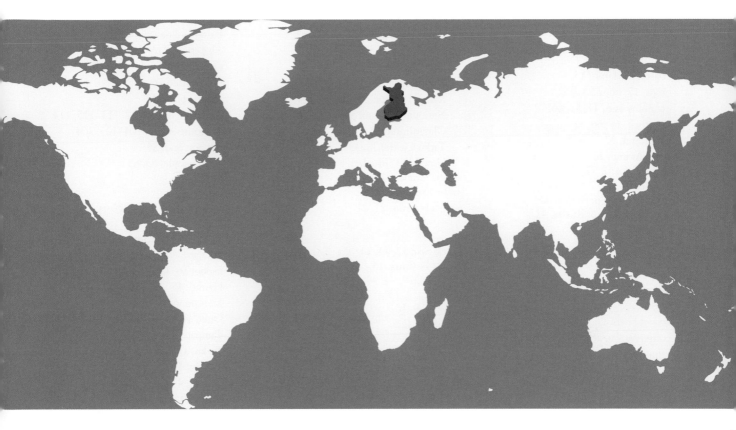

Index

Page numbers in *italics* indicate illustrations.

Meet the Author

GERI CLARK HAS BEEN WRITING NONFICTION FOR MIDDLE school audiences for twenty years. Most of her work focuses on science and mathematics, but she loves the opportunity to dive into something different. Writing a book like this should be an adventure. She relished the opportunity to explore a different culture and get to know new people. Reading the *Kalevala*, watching Finnish news broadcasts, listening to Finnish heavy metal, playing Finnish video games, and speaking to teachers in Finnish schools helped her learn about Finland in a way that made the country come alive. Clark is also lucky to have a few close Finnish friends who provided invaluable insight into what's important to Finns and what makes them tick.

Clark is a graduate of Cornell University and the New York University School of Journalism. Her work has appeared in many classroom publications including Scholastic *Science World* and *Scholastic MATH*.

Photo Credits